D0200692

SEEDS OF PEACE

SEEDS OF PEACE

*Contemplation
and Nonviolence*

by

WILLIAM H. SHANNON

A Crossroad Book
THE CROSSROAD PUBLISHING COMPANY
NEW YORK

1996
The Crossroad Publishing Company
370 Lexington Avenue, New York, NY 10017

Copyright © 1996 by William H. Shannon

All rights reserved. No part of this book may be reproduced,
stored in a retrieval system, or transmitted, in any form or by any means,
electronic, mechanical, photocopying, recording, or otherwise,
without the written permission of
The Crossroad Publishing Company.

Printed in the United States of America

Library of Congress Cataloging-in-Publication Data

Shannon, William Henry, 1917–
    Seeds of peace : reflections on contemplation and nonviolence /
by William H. Shannon.
        p.   cm.
    Includes bibliographical references.
    ISBN 0-8245-1557-9; 0-8245-1548-X (pb)
    1. Contemplation.   2. Nonviolence–Religious aspects–
Christianity.   I. Title.
BV5091.C7S47   1996
248.3'4–dc20   95-44249
                                                              CIP

Contents

❡

It is the Seedtime of Peace
—Zechariah 8:12 (NAB)

Peace is the seed-bed
of righteousness
and peacemakers
will reap its harvest.
—James 3:18 (REB)

Keeping Things in Perspective

❡

I am so happy for you. You will have the grace to see
through all that is inconsequential and unfortunate in the
Church. She is still the Body of Christ. . . . You are called to
a totally new, risen, transformed life in the Spirit of Christ.
—Thomas Merton to a person recently
received into the church

In one of his books, Frank Sheed speaks of a man whose
enthusiasm in believing God's revelation knew no bounds. He
is supposed to have said, almost wistfully, about the Trinity:
"Wish there were four of them so that I could believe in more
of them." Such a "faith" that stressed quantity over quality is
not an uncommon phenomenon in the Christian churches.
Christians do indeed believe a lot of things, and Roman
Catholics probably more than most. The Christian community,
as it has traveled through history, has picked up doctrinal statements, moral commitments, traditions, devotions, practices,
diverse national customs, and slews of causes, crusades, and
movements. As we look at this bewildering accumulation of all
sorts of religious baggage, we instinctively realize that certain
things are at the heart of the Christian reality, so much so that
without them that reality would cease to be what it is and turn
into something else. On the other hand, it seems equally clear
that there are ever so many things that are quite simply periph-
eral. Some of these have fallen into disfavor and been dropped
along the way. Yet all too many continue to be part of the bag-

gage we carry, even when they have ceased to have meaning or relevance. A lingering nostalgia wants to hang on to them, simply because they have been with us so long.

Every once in a while it behooves us to do some ecclesial housecleaning and take a hard look at this Christian "thing" and its components and rediscover what really matters and what does not. This means facing the question: What is the foundational reality against which we have to measure everything we think we are committed to believe and to do? To put it another way, What is the linchpin of Christian faith, without which the wheel falls off the axle and the pilgrim journey comes to an abrupt halt? This sorting-out process is important for all Christian churches. It is perhaps especially important for Roman Catholics, because we have gone through a period in our corporate life during which we seemed to be giving equal importance (or almost that) to everything that has ever been taught, believed, or practiced in the church.

The church is something like a tree. All the living parts of the tree are joined to the roots that ground the tree and give the rest of the tree its life and energy. The trunk is most immediately connected with the roots and hence quite necessary for the tree, if it is to retain its identity. There are big limbs that grow out from the trunk and carry a number of branches and leaves. If one of them is cut off, the tree can keep its essential identity, but something of its integrity is lost. Then there are the smaller branches and their leaves. Some of them can be lopped off without doing any harm to the tree; in fact, getting rid of them might well improve the appearance of the tree and its ability to grow.

Besides those things that are related to the roots, whether closely or remotely, there are various alien elements that have somehow become attached to it, though they have no relationship to the roots. Thus, in the course of time winds or storms may have affixed various things to the tree—sometimes things that make the tree look rather unsightly. Or birds may have come and built their nests in the tree. These nests serve an important need—for the birds; but they have nothing to do with the essence or the integrity of the tree.

The Second Vatican Council was, among other things, an effort on the part of the Catholic Christian community to look with a critical eye at this Christian tree that has grown through the ages (and accumulated an enormous amount of excess baggage, to switch to another metaphor) and try to discover the following: (1) What are the roots in which the whole thing is grounded? (2) What elements belong to its very essence? (3) What elements are necessary to preserve its integrity or wholeness?

Perspective-giving Directives

Did the council succeed in this task? Probably not. Certainly not entirely. What it did succeed in doing was to offer some important perspective-giving directives; for instance, its insistence that, when we think of church, we think first of the baptized rather than of the ordained, or its urgent concern that the church not only speak to the world but listen to it as well. The church, the council felt, must enter into dialogue with the world about fundamental questions relating to meaning, freedom, justice, and the many issues about which members of the human community can learn from one another, no matter how disparate their religious stances. Other examples could be given of this kind of sorting out achieved by the council, but there is much yet to be done. It may well be, however, that the council's most important accomplishment was its gift to the church of a clear principle to guide us in this ongoing task of sifting and sorting. The principle, found in the Decree on Ecumenism, reads as follows:

> When comparing doctrines [we must] remember that in Catholic teaching there exists an order or "hierarchy" of truths, since they vary in their relationship to the foundation of the Christian Faith. (art. 11)

In reflecting on this text, I decided to check the original Latin and discovered a slightly different emphasis from the above English translation. What is a *verb* in the translation ("vary") is actually an *adjective* in the original. Thus, the Latin says, more literally, that each of the doctrines taught by the church has a different connection (*diversus sit earum nexus*) with the foundation of Christian faith. The point of the principle, of course, is that the closer the connection, the higher place a particular doctrine enjoys in that "order" of teachings. And it is equally true that the farther away a particular teaching is from the foundation, the less importance we ought to attach to it. The trunk is closest to the roots. The limbs branching from the trunk come next. Then there are the smaller branches and the leaves. When you get to the debris that over time has somehow clung to the tree, there is no connection at all.

If I may change the metaphor from an ordinary tree out in the woods to a family tree, think of your parents as your human origins, the roots from which you spring. You would be close to those origins, as would be your siblings. Your own children and those of your siblings would also be closely connected to the origins. But when you get to second cousins once or twice removed and to in-laws, you are getting farther and farther away from your roots or, if you will, your "foundation." Your mother-in-law's great aunt would be so far removed that she would not figure in the family tree at all.

To get out of the trees (forest or family) and back to the principle (the varied degree of importance enjoyed by different things taught in the church depending on closeness of their relationship to the *foundation* of the Christian faith), our first task in applying this principle, in doing this sorting out, is to identify what the foundational truth actually is. Until we know that, it is impossible for us to arrange various doctrines into that "order or hierarchy," of which the council speaks. We have to locate the roots to find out what the trunk, the limbs, the branches depend on.

> *My, what a big tree*
> *You have!*

Too big, you think?
Well, Now that
You mention it . . .
Where should we start
Pruning?
Ask the tree. It
Will know.

The Foundational Truth

To discover the foundational truth, we need to go back to the beginnings and find out how Christian faith initially came into being. To put it in simplest form: in the beginning there was the *KERygma*. Most people have undoubtedly heard the word, but often in its mispronounced form *kerYGma*. The word, however you choose to pronounce it, means "proclamation." Our contemporary form of that proclamation is the acclamation of the eucharistic prayer at Mass: "Christ has died; Christ is risen; Christ will come again." Its most primitive form, spoken by heavenly voices to women beside an empty tomb, was simple and earth-shaking: "Why do you seek the living among the dead? *He is not here; he has been raised.*" The women were commissioned to take this glorious proclamation to the men who were the leaders among the followers of Jesus. But these men were no more willing to accept women's testimony than a Jewish court of the time would have been.

They were not disposed to believe until the upper room, securely locked for safety reasons by fearful and disillusioned disciples, was invaded by the Risen One himself. One can wonder whether or not the first words he spoke to them, when he so suddenly broke into their midst, might have been words of gentle rebuke, chiding them for refusing to accept the witness he had already sent to them, namely, the witness of the women. Perhaps he may have spoken in the following fashion:

My friends, I have already sent you the good news that God raised me from the dead into immortal life. Why did you refuse to listen to the women? Quite clearly, you have yet to learn that among my disciples there is neither Jew nor Gentile, free or slave, male or female. All have equal dignity and equal rights. It will always be to the glory of Mary Magdalene, Mary the mother of James and Joseph, and Salome and the other women that they were the first to announce the *kerygma,* and it will be to your shame that you refused to believe them.

This is, of course, my interpolation—though not entirely unwarranted, I would maintain, if one considers what the Gospels have to say about the manner in which Jesus dealt with women. At any rate, with or without a chiding, he joyfully gives them his peace and his Spirit. He shows them his wounds and sits down to share a meal with them. Thus it was that in the upper room they experience the substance of the *kerygma:* God had raised Jesus from the dead, and Jesus was alive with a life over which death had no more control.

The *kerygma,* experienced first by the women disciples and then by the men, is what the newborn church (which didn't even know yet that it was a church) began to preach and has continued to preach. This Easter event, the death-resurrection of Jesus, is the proclamation that is at the very heart of Christian faith. Read Peter's sermons in the early chapter of the Acts of the Apostles. The centerpiece of every one of them is this: *People put Jesus to death. God raised him up to new life, a new life that he shares with us.* This is the foundational truth: the resurrection of Jesus and its consequences for him and for us. Without the resurrection, Jesus would be a man of the past who once went about doing good, but who now would be very, very dead; and because he would be dead we would still be in our sins. With the resurrection as the foundation stone of the Christian edifice, he lives a new and immortal life; and the possibilities of that life are open to us, because he is, in the words of St. Paul, "the firstborn of many brothers [and sisters]." Everything else flows from this foundational truth and is to be judged of greater or lesser importance precisely in terms of the closeness of its connection to this truth.

The Needs of the Christian Community

What realities of Christian faith and life are closest to this foundational truth? This is no easy question to answer. It may well be that there are several acceptable answers, and people may legitimately disagree on the answer. This is simply to say that there is a body of beliefs, experiences, and realities that are close to the foundational truth. All are important. What one chooses as closest to the foundational truth may vary with the needs of the Christian community at a particular time in history. Thus, the question of who Jesus Christ was and how he related to God seriously engaged the church of the fourth and fifth centuries. This is an example of one area, among others, wherein growth took place in the church—a growth that brought new understanding and different nuances to what Christians believed from the beginning.

Perhaps another way of putting the issue we are dealing with is to say that, while there is a body of beliefs closely related to the foundational belief, each age has certain needs that will call for emphasis on one or another of these beliefs.

Our age is an age of lost identity in which there is an unprecedented quest for life's meaning and for some sense of self-awareness and self-worth. It is also a time in which violence exists on a scale that would have been impossible in earlier ages. What are the truths closely related to the foundational truth that can help us *in our time* to achieve a sense of who we are and at the same time rid our world of the scourge of violence that is everywhere rampant and seems to continue to grow?

It is my belief that a sense of our oneness with God in Christ, manifested so clearly in the Fourth Gospel, and an imitation of the unconditional love revealed in the teachings and life of Jesus, can help us in the search for self-identity. Moving toward a deeper sense of who we are will enable us to live a more tranquil, caring existence, modeled on Jesus' life. This, in turn, will lead us to an involvement in the daunting task of eliminating from our world war and terrorism and the many forms of violence in our society.

This brings me to the topic of this book: reflections on contemplation and nonviolence. It was suggested to me that I would be better off not using the word nonviolence, because it has a negative connotation for many people. I have decided to use it, however, because I want to see it as a positive alternative to the many and varied forms of violence that exist in human society and in all sorts of human relationships. I hope that by the time you complete reading this book you will have a very positive understanding of nonviolence. I want to ask you, therefore, to think positively when you see the word: if you will, think unconditional or nonviolent love. I believe—though I have to say this is a fairly recent conviction—that contemplation and nonviolence [*practice thinking "unconditional love," as you read this*] are realities and experiences that are very close to the foundational truth of Christian faith.

I am, of course, aware that the terms *contemplation* and *nonviolence* do not occur in the scriptures or in the early tradition. But I have come to the conviction that the realities, though not the words, are there. Contemplation, as it has come to be understood in the Christian tradition, is a return to the paradisiacal state of union with God, which brings to fulfillment the redemptive act of Christ. It is the beginning of a level of consciousness, beyond ordinary consciousness, in which one begins to experience the reality of new life, of risen life. It is an experience of union with God and a realization of our oneness with our sisters and brothers. If contemplation gives us an experience of communion with God and with one another, nonviolence is an inner force telling us how, in the light of that experience, we ought to act toward one another. It calls us to the way of unconditional love that highlights the life, teachings, and death of Jesus the Christ.

Why Am I Writing This Book?

I must admit that I am surprised to be writing a book on contemplation and nonviolence. I remember talking with a colleague in the field of theology several years after the Vatican Council, which, we both agreed, had considerably modified what we were teaching and the way we were doing it. I asked her, "Are you sometimes surprised at what you are saying in class?" "Surprised?" she answered, "I'm shocked." That is something like my feeling in writing on contemplation and nonviolence.

A Bit of Personal History

When I was ordained to the priesthood many years ago, I, of course, had no idea what the future held for me. A general outline of the scenario I expected was that I would be an assistant pastor for quite a number of years (there were lots of priests in those days); then I would get a parish "of my own." [That's the way we talked about becoming a pastor. The notion that the parish belonged to the people and not to the pastor came out of Vatican II, and in those days there was not even the whiff of a suggestion that this gigantic upheaval in the Roman Catholic Church was but a couple of decades down the road.] I had no idea that I would never become a pastor, that I would become, instead, a college chaplain and a college professor. I say I had no idea this would happen, though I have to admit it was something I secretly hoped for. To be a priest and a teacher seemed to me an ideal combination and, without ever expecting it to become a reality, I allowed myself to dream of such a possibility. There were times when I was uncomfortable with this dream, because I thought that, since I was a priest, I ought to want to be a pastor. Fortunately for the relief of my uneasy conscience, it was a time when priests were told, not asked, to go to a particular assignment. So, when it came, I had no difficulty in accepting my appointment to Nazareth College of Rochester as the will of God mediated through the orders of my bishop. It was a dream come true.

I don't remember any other dreams I had then about my future, but one thing I can say with absolute certitude: never in my wildest dreams did I think I would be writing books about contemplation, much less giving retreats and talks telling people that a contemplative experience is something to which we are all called. In those days, if I thought of contemplation at all, the picture of a John of the Cross or a Teresa of Avila would loom up before me, but certainly not my own visage. Contemplatives were people specially gifted by God, offered to the rest of us for our admiration, but hardly for our imitation. I sometimes read the books they wrote, though I never believed I really understood them; and I surely had no idea they were talking to me or that they were extending an invitation. I had about as much chance, I believed, of making the ascent of Mount Carmel as of climbing to the top of Mount Everest.

But, however far removed I may have felt from the experience of contemplation in those days, I had at least heard about it. I dare say this was not true of the second of the two topics that are central to this book, namely, nonviolence [*one more reminder – think "unconditional love," when you hear this word*]. I don't remember ever having even heard the word when I was in the seminary. I feel quite sure that I had heard the term *pacifism*, but it would not have been a term that would have stirred my heart and won my enthusiastic approval. In the first place, I probably would have given pacifism a skeptical look, because pacifists were quite generally Protestants—and I was ordained in a very unecumenical time in the life of the Roman Catholic Church. Moreover, pacifists were people who shirked their duty to defend their country in a just war; and, while I'm terribly reluctant to admit it now, in those days I probably believed that any war my country was engaged in was a just war. I took for granted that the only approach to a conflict situation between nations was the time-honored theory of the just war. I have to say, however, that there was one group of people who were Roman Catholic and also committed to pacifism who pricked my conscience, if ever so slightly. I am referring to the Catholic Worker people, especially Dorothy Day. They were remarkably dedicated to the gospel and the care of the poor and were also staunch pacifists.

But, whatever associations the word "pacifism" may have conjured up in my mind, I am sure that the word "nonviolence" never made an appearance in my seminary curriculum. I can't even remember when it became a part of my vocabulary [*and I wonder if you can remember when it entered yours*]. Most probably, I think, I began to hear of it in the 1960s, during the struggle of black people for civil rights. I certainly knew that the word was used by Martin Luther King, Jr., to describe his approach to the civil rights struggle, and I probably knew that he got it from that spindly little man who wore little more than a white loin cloth and bewildered Britain's mightiest politicians, Mohandas Gandhi. [*He wasn't satisfied with the word "nonviolence" either, but more about that later*]

I guess I would have to say that nonviolence began to catch on as a serious interest in my life when I began doing research on Thomas Merton, and especially when, as general editor of the Merton letters, I began meeting some of the people who were his friends and correspondents, especially those among them who were ardently committed, as he was, to nonviolence. In fact, I can pinpoint the time when nonviolence, from being a conviction I admired in others, became a personal commitment for me.

A Visit With Hildegard Goss-Mayr

It was 10 August 1982. I was in Nyack, New York, and had come to interview an Austrian woman who was visiting there at the headquarters of the Fellowship of Reconciliation. Her name was Hildegard Goss-Mayr. My reason for wanting to interview her was that she had corresponded with Thomas Merton and on one occasion had visited him at Gethsemani. The interview was to be in the late afternoon and evening. During the day she was conducting a workshop for the FOR staff, which I was invited to attend. Goss-Mayr had just come from Nicaragua, where she had been working with nonviolent groups. She began the workshop with a moving meditation

based on a letter she had just received from a family in
Nicaragua whose lives were in constant jeopardy. Throughout
the day this petite, soft-spoken woman put to us ever so com-
pellingly the obligation of Christians to recover the nonviolent
attitudes of Jesus and to put them into practice.

When I interviewed her in the late afternoon and then at a
quiet dinner we shared, I was deeply moved as she told me, in
that simple, straightforward way that is characteristic of her,
her story and that of her husband, Jean. Nonviolence had been
very much a part of her upbringing, since her father was
involved in the founding of the International Fellowship of
Reconciliation. Her husband, Jean Goss (who died in 1991),
was French and fiery. He came to nonviolence not because of a
family background but because of an event that happened in a
prison camp during the Second World War. He had a deep religious experience in which he came to be aware of Jesus as
Absolute Love. After their marriage in 1958, Hildegard and
Jean spent their entire lives traveling the world, teaching and
practicing nonviolence, and many times suffering for it. They
spend a good bit of time in Latin America, especially Brazil.
On one occasion, when she was in São Paulo in Brazil, Hildegard was arrested by the authorities and placed in a torture
prison. When she was finally freed, the suffering poor of São
Paulo said to her: "Now you are one of us." Hildegard and Jean
worked in eastern and western Europe. They had been training
nonviolent groups in the Philippines, when the nonviolent revolution against Ferdinand Marcos took place.

I felt singularly privileged in meeting this tiny, fragile-look-
ing, wonderful woman. (Thomas Merton said of her: She is my
candidate for sainthood.) I was moved with a sense of awe and
reverence, as I realized I was talking with someone who lived
the gospel of love every day and who exhibited in herself and in
her actions the strength of nonviolence and unconditional
love.

After such a meeting I could never be quite the same. I had
seen in her something deeply spiritual that I had been looking

for without realizing it. I had read about nonviolence and thought about it; but in this encounter I was brought face to face with it embodied in a person. I began to realize that nonviolence was no longer something I could choose or reject. It was a commitment I had to make. That day was the beginning of a long and still arduous journey, but I have never doubted that this journey follows the footsteps of the nonviolent Jesus.

In two previous books on prayer, *Seeking the Face of God* and *Silence on Fire*, I wrote briefly about the link between contemplation and nonviolence. This book is intended to follow the other two and expand on that link. As in the other two books of this trilogy, Thomas Merton is my chosen mentor—though apart from the quotations from his writings, this book will present my own thinking. I have tried to filter Merton's words and thought through my own experiences and to articulate what I believe needs to be said. Moreover, I have not hesitated to disagree with Merton where I thought it necessary to do so. For instance, although I deeply admire the profound insights he offers on nonviolence, I fault him for clinging overmuch to the "just war" theory in his approach to war. In this respect, like so many of his contemporaries, he relied more on natural law than on the teaching of the gospel.

In *Seeking the Face of God*, I attempted to revive a very old way of approaching prayer and to put a contemporary dress on it. I made use of a twelfth-century work by Guigo the Carthusian, the *Scala Claustralium* (Ladder of Monks). I tried to show its relevance for any age and for people other than monks. The first two rungs of Guigo's ladder are reading the scriptures and meditating on them. These two steps up the ladder had as their purpose not so much the gaining of new knowledge as a kind of relocating of the Word of God. Their goal, in other words, is to move the Word from the mind to the heart. The heart in medieval thought was considered to be the center of the feelings and emotions and the source from which actions flowed. Words simply in the mind might tell one what Jesus said and did, but only the Word in the heart could move one to follow in Jesus' footsteps.

Once the Word is relocated at a person's center, it becomes a force that motivates to action. Hence, reading and meditation issue in crying out to God with words of praise, thanks, repentance, and supplication. They will also issue in actions that will serve the good of the community. (Guigo doesn't say this, but I did. And I doubt that Guigo would quarrel with me about it.) The third rung of the ladder, then, is prayer with words.

The fourth rung of the ladder, contemplation, is a bit trickier to deal with. It doesn't just flow out of the other three, as they seem to flow out of one another. Contemplation, which is a total awareness of God that takes us beyond all dualities and enables us to find ourselves where alone we are truly real—that is, in God—is a gift God gives us when we are ready for it. It isn't that God is teasing us, as if God were saying: "Just wait your turn. There are others ahead of you on the list." It's just that you can't fill a bottle with good wine if it's already full of poor wine. You first have to empty it so that it can receive the good wine. So we have to empty ourselves of a false and illusory self. Only when we are thus empty can God fill us with God's very self and enable us to find ourselves in God. When this happens in death, we have achieved heaven. When it happens in this life, we have achieved contemplation. When one has reached this point or is even beginning to approach it, we may rightfully speak of a contemplative spirituality, namely, a way of life lived in awareness of God and with alertness to God's presence.

After completing *Seeking the Face of God,* I came to realize that there was something missing. While I had said that contemplation was God's gift that we have to wait for, I had made no suggestions as to what we ought to be involved in while we are waiting. In other words, I needed to face the question, granted that contemplation is always a gift that we can never claim as our right, are there any things we can do to prepare and dispose ourselves to receive this gift? It was this question that spurred me to write *Silence on Fire.* Written for those I called "contemplatives-in-process," it was chiefly about what I called "the Prayer of Awareness." If contemplation was the highest point of our *vertical ascent* to God (our being lifted up to God by God), then the prayer of awareness—contemplation's humble relative—could be seen as the *horizontal steps* we take to help ready ourselves for that being lifted up. Prayer of awareness was the plane moving along the runway but powerless to raise itself into the air. Only God could pull the stick (or whatever it is that pilots do) to get us off the ground and into the air. To put it more simply, if contemplation is total awareness of God wherein we are completely absorbed in God, then the prayer of awareness is the various degrees of awareness, short of that total immersion in God, that we can more or less achieve on our own, with God's ordinary, garden-variety grace, so to speak. These different levels of awareness lighten us up so that we are ready for God when God scoops us up into God's very Self.

In both of these books I made the connection between prayer—especially contemplation—and nonviolence. But the emphasis was on prayer. Nonviolence was seen as a necessary consequence. For the more one becomes aware of God, the more nonviolence enters into the picture. For contemplation (and I want this term to include contemplation's more modest understudy, prayer of awareness) offers us an intuition of the oneness we have with one another in God: the intuition of a oneness that underlies our superficial differences. This intuition of necessity begets nonviolence, which is simply living that oneness in everyday situations. Moreover, it is not just that contemplation leads us to nonviolence; the practice of nonviolence at the same time deepens the contemplative perspective. It removes the destructive forces that tend to divide us, and thus it makes the unity we have with all our sisters and brothers shine all the brighter. We begin to live a spirituality that is both contemplative and nonviolent.

If we could personify contemplation and nonviolence, we could imagine Contemplation giving us a talk (though, of course, it never actually speaks—it is most eloquent in its silence—but we can pretend): "Let me show you that you are not an isolated individual. You are one with all your sisters and brothers in God." At this point Contemplation would hand the

microphone to Nonviolence. Nonviolence (not at all loath to
use words) would say to us: "So, contemplation has brought you
to an awareness of your oneness with all in God, has it? Now
you must strive to live that oneness in all your relationships.
Reach out to your sisters and brothers through the power of
unconditional love."

In this present book I want to continue pointing out this intimate connection, but I want to reverse the emphasis somewhat, giving more time to nonviolence as it impinges on our
entire moral life and all our relationships. I will see to it,
though, that contemplation is always present as an overseer,
making sure that nonviolence does not go astray.

The New *Catechism of the Catholic Church*

Roman Catholics have recently been recipients of a huge
compendium of Catholic belief, piety, and devotion called *The
Catechism of the Catholic Church*. Leafing through its eight hundred pages is proof enough, I believe, of what I said at the
beginning of this introduction: that we have picked up a *lot of
things*, as we have progressed through the centuries. I welcome
the catechism as the compendium it is intended to be. But its
sheer bulk makes me realize, all the more, how necessary it is
that we sort out and bring to the fore the few really fundamental things of our faith that are at the heart of it all.

Perhaps we could picture the material in the eight-hundred-
page catechism arranged in a great many circles around a center. If we are going to make sense out of these eight hundred
pages, we have to find the center of these many circles and see
every circle about that center as important insofar as it helps us
live at the center or from the center. At that center we find the
Risen Jesus with his new command of love. It is "new," for it is
not just a reprise of the Hebrew Scriptures' teaching about love
of God and neighbor: it is new because we are to love one
another, *as he has loved*. We have to "become" him and love with
his kind of love. What was his kind of love? It was an uncondi-

tional love. Unconditional in its *intensity:* he was willing to go wherever love would take him, even to laying down his life for his own. Unconditional in its *extension:* no one was excluded. He loved all women and men, not just his friends but also the outsiders, the aliens, even those who would be his enemies. It was unconditional too in its *motivation:* it refused any means of encountering another that was not motivated and sustained by love. This meant rejecting violence and any manipulation of others. It meant the deepest respect for the truth in the other person. Finally, it was unconditional in its *universality:* it burst the bonds of all legal systems that would try to restrict it. No legal system could contain it.

It is contemplation that enables us to live *at the center;* it is nonviolence [i.e., unconditional love] that enables us to live *from the center* and to move to various points on life's circumference that constitute our everyday relationships with people and with society's structures.

The prophet Zechariah lived at the end of the sixth century B.C.E. His prophetic book, written in a critical time in the life of his people, is a call for the rebuilding of the community of Israel and the ushering in of an era of peace. "It is," he writes, "the seedtime of peace" (Zech. 8:12, NAB). We live in times that are critical not just for our own country but for the whole universe. Unprecedented ways of destruction are available that could bring an end to human life on this planet. But there are also unprecedented resources for creating and preserving peace. Our time can be the "seedtime of peace." May this book on contemplation and nonviolence offer the seeds for the making of a truly peaceful world; for contemplation and nonviolence are truly the *Seeds of Peace.*

CHAPTER ONE

Thomas Merton and the Reshaping of American Catholic Spirituality

¶

> Perhaps I am called upon to objectify the truth that
> America, for all its evil, is innocent and somehow igno-
> rantly holy.
>
> —Thomas Merton, *Sign of Jonas*

In 1968 a young man wrote to Thomas Merton saying that he wanted to come to Gethsemani because he had been strongly attracted to Merton through his writings. Merton's advice to him was to pray and seek for God's will. "But don't," he said, "build on a mudpile like me! I just don't have disciples, don't look for disciples, and don't think I could be of any use to disciples. My suggestion to you is to be a disciple of Christ, not of any man" (*WTF*, 241–42).

Yet whether he liked it or not, Thomas Merton has been the spiritual director of many people who have found that the spirituality they discovered in his writings opened a whole new way of life for them. It reshaped their spirituality.

The Woman from Tucson

Some time ago I received a letter from a woman in Tucson who made precisely this point. She told me how Thomas Merton had changed her life. Now in her fiftieth year, she had grown up, she told me, "during a period in the church in which lay people were considered second-class members. Thomas Merton was the one who provided a breakthrough for me. It came in a section of his *Seven Storey Mountain,* in which he speaks of the contemplative vocation as one to which all are called (p. 419). It was the first time in my adult life," she went on, "in which the guilt of 'not following a religious vocation' fell away and I had permission (from my own spirit) to continue my journey to wholeness as a lay person."

Reflect with me for a moment on what this woman said. Merton transformed her understanding of spirituality. First, he freed her from a terrible guilt feeling: the feeling that, because she had not followed a call to enter the religious life, she had deliberately chosen a second-rate type of Christian living. Second, Merton taught her that her real vocation (and indeed that of every Christian) is the vocation to contemplation. Third—and perhaps most remarkable of all—the realization that she was indeed called to contemplation as a lay woman enabled her to stand on her own two feet and make her own decisions of conscience. The way she put it is instructive: "I had permission," she said, "to continue my journey to wholeness as a lay person." But note that the permission came not from Merton or from anyone else but from her own spirit. Contemplation brought her freedom, a new sense of personal autonomy in making decisions in her life. Finally, she knew that spiritually she could not stand still; she had to journey on— and the journey was toward personal wholeness.

Some of the convictions she arrived at through her experience of reading Merton are basic ingredients of a new way of thinking in the Catholic Church in the latter half of the twentieth century that has brought about a radical reshaping of American Catholic spirituality: the conviction (1) that she possessed equal citizenship with everyone else in the kingdom of God, (2) that she was called to contemplative union with God, (3) that she was conscious of a new-found freedom in making conscience decisions that were her own and not vicarious decisions made for her by someone else and, finally, (4) that spirituality meant not just prayer but the whole of life lived contemplatively and in process of continual growth toward personal wholeness and authenticity.

I want to discuss further the characteristics of this "new" spirituality. But first I want to say a few words about the "older" spirituality that this woman was brought up with and that was the heritage of most of us who lived parts of our lives in the first half of the twentieth century. Elsewhere (in *Silence on Fire*) I have called this spirituality a spirituality of devotion.

The Spirituality of Devotion: Memories from the Past

The basic premise of the spirituality of devotion was that the life of grace was a gift from God that I received in the sacraments and that I could foster by the performance of various acts of piety and devotion. In the days when this spirituality predominated, devotions were at their highest pitch: novenas, for instance, which came in many varieties. St. Joseph's Church in downtown Rochester, New York, stood for Catholics in my area as a symbol of this type of spirituality. Every Wednesday people flocked to St. Joseph's for the novena in honor of our Lady of Perpetual Help. Other parishes had different types of novenas. One of the most popular was the Miraculous Medal novena (an odd sort of devotion when you think of it—devotion to a medal). We had this at Sacred Heart Cathedral when I was assigned there as a newly ordained priest in 1943. We held our novena on Tuesday nights, but no one could really compete with St. Joseph's. They packed people in several times on Wednesdays. In terms of numbers, their novena won out, hands down, over all the others. In fact, several nearby restaurants prospered because the novena-goers became steady customers. Perhaps part of the reason for the gradual demise of downtown Rochester was that St. Joseph's Church burned down. [Were the culprits maybe another novena group wanting to do away with the competition?] The façade of St. Joseph's Church was all that survived the fire; it was preserved as a city landmark. This façade, with the body of the church gone, stands as a mute reminder of a spirituality that to a great extent is disappearing.

But to return again to that spirituality. Going to Mass was swept up into this devotional mentality. Being at Mass was not the action of a community united to praise God; it was another form of devotion. People went to Mass to say their prayers, occasionally adverting to what the priest was doing at the altar. Thus, everyone stopped saying their prayers when the moment of the consecration came. During this moment they watched what the priest did, but then they returned to their rosaries or prayer books. People said all sorts of prayers during Mass. Thirty-days prayers were popular. So were the accumulated prayer cards people had stuck in their prayer books, and of course prayers that had indulgences attached to them were particularly valuable. They offered a two-for-one value that one would be foolish to pass up.

When you think of it, the Mass of yesteryear must have appeared odd to an uninitiated stranger who happened into a Catholic church at Mass time: seeing the priest up in front doing his bit and the choir in the back doing theirs and the rest of the people saying their rosaries or reading their prayer books. The three groups—clergy, choir, people—would appear to be quite unconnected. They certainly would not appear as a community doing something together.

This spirituality of devotion was a spirituality that put great store on *doing things:* doing things that were pleasing to God or, more ominously, doing things to placate God if I thought I had failed to please *him.* It seemed to be a basic principle that the harder something was, the more it must please God.

It was, moreover, a spirituality that felt quite sure that God wasn't very easy to please. Almost certainly, if several weeks had gone by, you must have done a fair number of things that displeased God. Hence, off to the confessional box. Scripture might say that the fear of God leads to wisdom; for all too many it led to the confessional. For some people, there were almost as many confessions as communions. For the most rigid, it was one communion *on* one confession. Then back to the box again before another communion. For the very sensitive this spirituality often generated scrupulosity: that terrible, frightful, nagging feeling that one never did anything that was pleasing to God. God was always lurking around the corner waiting to catch you in sin.

> *In the confessional*
> *Is darkness.*
> *The priest sees*
> *No one. And no one*
> *Sees the priest.*
> *What happens*
> *If the priest says*
> *The words, and no one*
> *Is there?*

But all of these devotional practices were, in great measure, exterior to daily life, which was clearly secular and worldly. Hence, they had little effect on the rest of one's life, in contrast to contemplation, which permeated the lives of those who were called to it. And everyone knew that such people were either in convents or monasteries: there were no contemplatives in the world and no possibility of contemplation there. This seemed to be especially the case with people who were married. It is true that one could read stories of saints who were married and did achieve the heights of contemplative life, for example, St. Elizabeth of Hungary. But the interesting thing about her story (and the stories of others in similar positions who also reached high levels of spirituality) is that she was able to do this only as a widow. It was only after she buried her husband that she could devote herself to contemplative spirituality.

Devotional spirituality placed a high premium on getting forgiveness for wrongdoing rather than on conversion to a deeper union with God. It was therefore a static spirituality: my response to religious imperatives was the same at the age of fifty as it had been at the age of twenty. Spiritually it was enough to stand still, concerned not to fall back into old sinful ways but not really thinking of growing and moving ahead. It could hardly be called a spirituality of growth to wholeness and maturity.

It was a privatized spirituality. My great task in life was to save my own soul. The fires of social responsibility burned very low. I may have practiced the corporal and spiritual works of mercy, but I probably did so not because I had a burning desire to change society for the better but because I was quite sure that good works like these would please God and thus enable me to save my soul, even as I helped others to do the same for themselves. It was very much of an otherworldly spirituality: poor banished children of Eve, we sent up our sighs, mourning and weeping in this vale of tears, hoping that after this our exile we might enter at last into our heavenly home.

The Root Problem

I could say much more about this spirituality of devotion (and I have already said a good bit about it in *Silence on Fire*). It was a spirituality that I lived for a good part of my life and I don't mean to mock it; for many people it was the only kind of spiritual life they ever knew. But perhaps the one most important thing that needs to be said about it is this: the root problem of this spirituality was that it produced in so many people a warped, cramped, crippled understanding of God. The God of this spirituality was not the God whom Jesus Christ revealed to us. This God was not that hidden ground of love in whom we all live and move and have our being. At worst he (and I use the word "he" advisedly, because the God of this spirituality was very clearly a patriarchal God) was a tyrant God who punished us relentlessly when we were bad and somewhat arbitrarily (at least so it seemed at times) dolled out favors to us when we were good. At best he was a God aloof from us. His abode was in heaven; we were on earth, and he watched us from afar. This notion of God flowed from a dualistic understanding of reality. It was what I have called in *Silence on Fire* a spirituality of apartheid. Political apartheid separates blacks from whites; spiritual apartheid separates God from God's creation. God was there and the world was here. The most radical problem with this spirituality was that it stressed the transcendence of

God (namely, that God is infinitely above and beyond all that is created) but ignored God's immanence (namely, that God was in all things and that all things were in God).

The "Will of God" was embodied in the external dictates of impersonal laws. As Merton puts it, God's will was "a sphinx-like and arbitrary force bearing down on us with implacable hostility." Such an understanding of God's intents only leads people "to lose faith in a God they cannot find it possible to love. . . . These arbitrary 'dictates' of a domineering and insensible Father are more often seeds of hatred than of love." Merton goes on to say that such an understanding of God's will would make impossible the intimate encounter that takes place in contemplation. "We will," Merton says, "desire only to fly as far as possible from Him and hide from His Face forever." He goes on to offer an important perspective-giving statement: "So much depends on our idea of God!" (NSC, 15).

Introducing Contemplative Spirituality

But I don't want to spend a lot of time flaying a spirituality that has either disappeared from the scene or at the very least has significantly waned in importance. I want to talk about the spirituality that, to a large degree, has replaced it. This new spirituality, which I call "contemplative spirituality," was in no small measure Thomas Merton's gift to the Christian community. I say it was his gift not because he invented it but because he rescued it from the marginal position it had occupied in Catholic thinking and practice and placed it at the center of our understanding of spirituality.

This contemplative spirituality is not a wholescale revolt against the spirituality of the past. It accepts the importance of devotions and the sacraments in our lives. Its most radical point of difference lies in the way it understands God, and it is to this topic that I now turn.

CHAPTER TWO

Who Is the God
of Contemplative Spirituality?

¶

So much depends on our idea of God! No idea of Him, however pure and perfect, is adequate to express Him as He
really is. Our idea of God tells us more about ourselves than
about God.

—Thomas Merton, *NSC*

God is not experienced as an object outside ourselves, as
"another being" capable of being enclosed in some human
concept.

—Thomas Merton, *HGL*

So much does indeed depend on our "idea of God." Contemplative spirituality, like any theistic spirituality, is rooted in the
truth of the transcendence of God. But it steadfastly refuses to
identify the transcendence of God with a vision of God guid-
ing and sustaining the universe and the world of people from
afar. For contemplative spirituality, God is the mystery that is at
the heart of all reality. God is somehow united with the true
self that is in every person. God is in a relationship of closest
intimacy with everyone who is.

Our Idea of God and
Our Understanding of Prayer

Our idea of God strongly influences the way we live our lives,
and what I am interested in at the moment is the way it influences how we think of prayer. Most of us, I am sure, recall the

catechism definition of prayer as "the lifting up of the mind and heart to God." What Merton points out—and this is at the very core of contemplative spirituality—is that "prayer is not only the 'lifting up of the mind and heart to God'" but also, and most especially, "the response to God within us, the discovery of God within us; it leads ultimately to the discovery and fulfillment of our own true being in God" (introduction to a book of selected prayers given to the choir novices, Lent 1961, unpublished).

Now discovering God within us should not be misunderstood. We must not think of God as a kind of little being inside us with whom we can get in touch. No, what we need to realize is that we simply must not conceive of God as an object or a being. In *New Seeds of Contemplation,* Merton writes: "There is 'no such thing' as God, because God is neither a 'what' nor a 'thing' but a pure 'Who.' He is the 'Thou' before whom my inmost 'I' springs into awareness [and love. He is the living God, Yahweh, 'I AM,' who calls us into existence out of nothing, so that we stand before Him in His image and reflecting His infinite being in our littleness and reply. 'I am.'"] (p. 13). [I have put the last part in brackets, because this was an addition Merton made to the French text.]

God, Merton is telling us, is the One who calls all things and objects into existence. That is what things and objects and persons are: beings called into existence by God. Since God has brought them into existence, God is not one of them. God cannot be placed among the beings he has brought into existence. God, therefore, is not a thing. God is no-thing. But all things are in God because God calls them into being and sustains them in being. When God spoke to Moses in the scene of the burning bush, God identified Who God was. God said: "I am." Now, because God has given me existence, I too can say: "I am." But what we must be clear about is that this smallest of all sentences does not mean the same thing when I say it as when God says it. God says: "I am" in total independence. He needs nothing, no one, to enable God to say "I am." I say "I am," but it is an "I am" that is radically dependent on the "I am" of God. A

cartoon that appeared in *Commonweal* some time ago said this
so delightfully. It shows God speaking to all creation and saying: "I am; therefore you are."

Radical Dependence

What does it mean to say that my "I am" is radically dependent on God's? It means dependence in my very roots. It means
that I am so totally dependent on God for my being that apart
from God I would simply cease to be. It means that when my
nothingness intersects with God's infinite reality, I experience
God at the heart of that nothingness. A newborn child is
dependent on her mother, and we almost take it for granted
that a mother would never be forgetful of her child. Isaiah puts
it this way: "Can a woman forget the infant at her breast or a
mother the child of her womb?" His implied answer is: "Of
course not." Then, speaking God's words, Isaiah says: "But
should even these forget, I shall never forget you" (49:15, REB).

These words express not only the divine compassion; they
also express an ontological truth. We are so radically dependent
on God that if God were to forget us for an instant, we would
simply cease to be. If a mother forgot about her baby girl, one
would hope that someone else would take care of her. But if
God were to forget us, we would, quite simply, vanish into nothingness. To express this in a more positive way: when we truly
meet God at the point where our nothingness intersects with
God's infinite reality, we experience God at the heart of our
nothingness. And *we know that we are only because God is.* We
know that we are contemplatives, for we have experienced who
we are in God. We have experienced *that of God which is in us*
and which alone is truly and ultimately real. This truth is so central that we shall return to it several times and in different ways.

The Greatness of God

At this point you might want to say: "You are confusing me.
One minute you say God is no thing. God is no being. Then

you talk about God in very personal terms, expressing God's relationship to us in terms of a tender maternal relationship. I must object that you are not giving me the clear notion of God I expected you to give." In response I would have to say: "You are right. I haven't given you a clear, definite picture of who God is. I haven't done so because I can't." For we are here faced with a theme about God that the Scriptures (especially the psalms) never tire of returning to: namely, the greatness of God that exceeds any human greatness we can conceive of or describe. "Great is the Lord and wholly to be praised" (Ps. 48:1). "For you are great and you do wondrous things" (Ps. 86:10). "O Lord, my God, you are great indeed!" (Ps. 104:1).

The greatness of God is a frequent topic also in Christian hymnody. The hymn that almost immediately comes to mind is "How Great Thou Art." There was a time when Catholics would have disdainfully dismissed this hymn as "Protestant," but in recent years it has become very popular in Catholic worship. Some weeks ago a priest-friend of mine told me of a non-liturgical setting he had discovered for that hymn: every morning as he shaves and sees himself in the mirror, the words come spontaneously to his lips: "How great thou art!" Whatever you might want to say about my friend's need to cultivate a bit more humility, it is important to understand that his extra-liturgical use of this hymn has drastically changed the meaning of the word "great." No one, including my boastful friend, is great as God is great.

The word "great" applied to God takes on a meaning radically different from the meaning it has when applied to humans. Thus it would be true to say that God is "great," because something of what we consider "great" in humans is in God; at the same time it would be equally true to say that God is "not great," because the puny greatness of creatures is as nothing compared to the greatness of God. It isn't simply that God has a lot more greatness than we could possibly have; rather God's greatness absolutely transcends whatever we might call greatness in any human person. All this is to say that when we talk about God, we have to use the *superlative* (God's greatness, goodness, and so on far exceed these qualities in humans) or the *negative* (these qualities which we see in creatures exist in them in a way that is so limited and impoverished that it makes sense to deny that they even exist in God, i.e., in that limited and impoverished way).

Meister Eckhart to the Rescue

Meister Eckhart, the fourteenth-century Rhenish mystic, with that lucid ambiguity so characteristic of him, describes the radical difference between God and us in this way. He says: "The Divine One is a negation of negations and a denial of denials." He goes on to clarify: "Every creature contains a negative, namely, a denial that it is the other. God contains the denial of denials. God is the One who denies of every other that it is anything except Himself."

What he is saying is that every creature is finite, which is to say that it is limited in what it is. A particular creature is only "this"; it is not "that." It is their limited being that distinguishes one creature from another. To say that a tree is a tree is to deny that it is a bird or a rock or any other created thing. This is what Eckhart means when he tells us that every creature contains a negative: a denial that it is the other.

After telling his congregation [these words, I should point out, are from one of his sermons! How would you like to belong to his congregation?] that every creature is a denial that it is anything other than itself, he goes on to speak about God and says that God is a denial of denials. First, God is a denial that He/She is "this" or "that." Now "this" or "that" represents each and every created reality: a tree, a stone, a bird, a flower, a woman, a man, and so on. This seems clear enough: because God is God—that is, the One who transcends all created reality—God is a denial that He/She is anything that we experience in the created world. God is not to be located among creatures. We can imagine lining up all created objects, things, persons.

God could not be one of them, for God transcends all created beings.

But Eckhart says more (and now things get really complicated!): God is a denial of denials. In other words, God is a denial that God is *not* "this"; God is a denial that God is *not* "that"; God is a denial that God is *not* any and every creature that exists. Does this sound pretty heavy? Try thinking of it in this way. Eckhart is saying that, while God *is not* "this" or "that," there is yet a sense in which God *is* "this" and "that" and indeed "is" every creature that exists—not in any pantheistic way, but in the sense that, apart from God, neither "this" nor "that" nor any creature could exist. Why? Because God is the Source and Ground of each and every creature that is. Every "this," every "that," every creature exists only because it finds its being, identity and uniqueness in God. Apart from God, it simply could not be.

[A tip (as they say in the computer instruction books): Eckhart is saying there are two negatives in God. The first (stating that God is not "this" or "that") affirms the divine transcendence, namely, that God is above and beyond all created reality. The second (stating in a negative way the positive truth that God is the Ground of all that exists) affirms the divine immanence, namely, that God is in everything and that everything is in God.]

Let's Face It: God Is Mystery

At this point you may feel, once again, a bit let down, maybe even exasperated and might want to say: "Look, you told me that the God of devotional spirituality was not the true God. Ok, you may be correct, but whether true or not at least people knew what they meant when they used the word 'God.' You are talking about another spirituality, which you call contemplative. Why doesn't it offer me a clearer notion of God? But you are telling me that it can't. You're fogging the issue. Instead of helping me to understand God better, you are making God more of a mystery than ever." My answer would be: "Quite so. This is precisely what I want to do: enable you to live comfortably with the truth that God is Mystery."

There is a person to whom I have been giving spiritual direction for some time. Gradually I have encouraged her to do less thinking and less discursive reasoning in her private prayer and to spend more time in wordless prayer. On one occasion she said to me: "I used to think of prayer as friendly conversation with God. I imagined God at my side and myself speaking with God as I would with a friend. Now, while I know that that is a legitimate metaphor for prayer (and there are times when I still find it useful), more and more in my private prayer, I feel the need of going beyond images and words. Strangely, as I have let myself be drawn more and more in this direction, I have found that God has become more and more a mystery to me. Yet unaccountably I feel there is more depth in my prayer. I really experience that I am touching God or, perhaps better, that I am being touched by God."

Thomas Merton, in the booklet of prayers for the Gethsemani novices that I referred to earlier in this chapter, wrote: "To pray is to enter into mystery, and *when we do not enter into the unknown, we do not pray.* If we want everything in our prayer-life to be abundantly clear at all times, we will by that very fact defeat our prayer-life."

Perhaps, dear reader, I may be disappointing you. You may be thinking: "If God is mystery—and there just is no satisfying answer to the question Who is God?—then why bother talking about God at all?" Maybe the reason for your disappointment, if indeed that is your reaction, is that you think of mystery as something that must be solved.

The Excitement of Mystery

But I would suggest that calling God mystery amounts to extending an invitation to the endless excitement of probing ever more deeply into the reality of God, though with the realization that one will never be able to exhaust the meaningfulness of God. To call God mystery is to remind ourselves that *all the knowledge we have of God comes from some human experience of God*. The heart of the mystery is this: *the words we possess are able to express only the human experience, not the divine reality experienced*. That is why all the language we use about God is metaphorical. When we speak about God we are always using analogies. We have no divine language, only human.

> *Analogy means*
> *When I say God*
> *Is this,*
> *I must also say God*
> *Is not this. Why, then,*
> *Don't I*
> *Just say*
> *Nothing?*
> *Because God*
> *Gave me words.*

St. Gregory of Nyssa May Help

St. Gregory of Nyssa has a striking comparison in one of his homilies that can help us understand something of this problem, which is at once agonizing and yet alluring: The unknowability of God seeming to thwart the immense desire we have to know God. Gregory describes the way of light and the way of darkness. He pictures a high mountain on the edge of the sea. The mountain is split in two with a sheer drop from top to bottom. At the top a ledge projects out from the mountain and enables me to look down. I can look down only for a short time because looking down gives me a feeling of dizziness. My looking down into the depths may be likened to human faculties striving to know God all by themselves. We look into those depths and when the sun is out we catch some glimpses of what is there. And we can put words on it, though the words are never adequate. But when the sun sets and darkness descends, the depths below the mountain are enshrouded in complete darkness. We only know that they are there because we have had some experience of them in the light.

We have to let go of the ledge. We have to make a leap of faith and jump into the abyss of the darkness below. God catches us in God's divine arms, even though God has no arms. Now we are no longer just looking at the depth from a distance. We are plunged into the depths, into God. We experience God because we realize that we are in God and always have been, but we didn't know it until we took that leap of faith. Yet having taken it, we are powerless to put the experience into words.

As this desire to talk about God confronts the impossibility of doing so, we readily identify with the sentiments of the prophet Jeremiah:

> If I say, "I will not mention Him,
> Or speak any more in His name,"
> then within me there is something like a burning fire
>   shut up in my bones.
> I am weary with holding it in,
>   and I cannot. (20:9, NRSV)

As the Sufi mystics would put it: when a person comes to know God, his/her tongue is silent. When a person knows, he or she does not speak; for what they know transcends the capabilities of what they are able to say. Yet, as Merton points out, there is a strong tendency to use words to express what we experience. But, unfortunately, what happens is that the words break asunder that deep communion that lies beyond words. Voicing the words means losing the experience.

Becoming a Blind Lion

In 1949, Merton had a book of poems published, called *The Tears of the Blind Lions.* The title was based on a quotation from the French novelist Leon Bloy: "When those who love God try to talk about Him, their words are blind lions looking for

springs in the desert." I would suggest that there is a hint of
autobiography in the choice of that title. Merton was himself
one of the blind lions loving God and trying to talk about him.
He was a *lion,* because of the immense inner resources he possessed. But he was a *blind lion* because, in spite of his great
inner strength and his unquestionable literary talents, he knew
that he could never adequately articulate the contemplative
experience. In fact, in the last year of his life, he wrote:

> I don't really want to write about "spiritual things." . . . I have
> gradually developed a nausea about talking about contempla-
> tion. Except when I really have to. The words sound too empty
> and trivial. I just don't like spinning out a lot of words about God
> and prayer. I feel in fact immensely poor and fallible, but I don't
> worry about it. I just live. (*SC,* 323)

Before he came to write this statement, he had already spun
out a lot of words about contemplation; no matter how inadequate he felt the words were, we are all the richer for them.

The Tears of the Blind Lions contains a poem modeled on
Psalm 137, the psalm of the Jewish exiles in Babylon, weeping
as they remembered Zion, the holy city, and its temple:

> If I forget you, O Jerusalem,
> let my right hand wither!
> Let my tongue cling to the roof of my mouth,
> if I do not remember you.
> if I do not set Jerusalem
> above my highest joy. (Ps. 137:5–6, NRSV)

In his variation on the theme of the psalm, Merton identifies
the city of Zion with contemplation and the Jerusalem temple
with the inner recesses of the self where one confronts God.
Thus:

> May my bones burn and ravens eat my flesh,
> If I forget thee, contemplation!
> May language perish from my tongue,
> If I do not remember thee, O Zion, city of vision.
>
> (*TBL,* 20)

Note the final phrase of the poem—"city of vision." The lion is blind, yet at the same time he is in the "city of vision." The reason the contemplative is blind is not that there is no light, but rather that the brilliance of God who "dwells in unapproachable light" is so dazzling that it puts out all lesser lights (human reason, human words). Thus, in one sense the contemplative does not see, because he or she is blinded by the light of God. In another sense the contemplative is a person of vision who sees what others do not see. On the very first page of his book *New Seeds of Contemplation* Merton writes: "In contemplation we know by 'unknowing.' Or, better, we know *beyond* all knowing or 'unknowing.'" William James, in his *Varieties of Religious Experience,* says much the same thing. The mystical experience, he tells us, is "ineffable" (it cannot be "effed"; it cannot be put into words). Yet at the same time it is noetic: the mystic really knows with an unusual clarity what he or she did not know before.

More than that, the contemplative is in touch with what is really real in a way that other people are not. That is why the vision of the contemplative is so important for today's world. He or she knows and in some way experiences the love and the compassion that exist at the heart of all reality.

The Tenderness of God

Earlier I voiced another objection that I thought might have come to your mind, namely, that in one paragraph I was stating quite definitively that God was no thing, and then in the very next paragraph, I was speaking of God in very tender relational terms. Well, let's take a look at that seeming inconsistency, remembering all the while that language about God is always the language of metaphors. Think of the many *names of God* that we find in the Bible: Savior, Redeemer, Deliverer, Refuge, Helper, Shepherd, Ruler, Mother, Father, Lover, and so on. If we reflect on them, we note that they are all *relational:* we relate to God as the One who is our Source and Sustainer, the One who cares for us and provides for us, a God of tenderness and compassion. This is to say that *we are talking about a God who loves us.*

When the scriptures say (as the author of the Fourth Gospel never tires of saying) that "God is Love," they are drawing on a human experience: all of us, one would hope, love and are loved. Now love is the deepest of all human mysteries. We can experience it, but we cannot adequately explain what it is we are experiencing. Hence, when we say "God is Love," we are not resolving the mystery of God; rather we are touching the mystery of God with another mystery. Love is as incomprehensible as God. Still, we have experiences of love in our lives, and these experiences can help us understand a little more clearly who God is.

In one of his reading notebooks, Merton quotes a saying of Allah attributed to the prophet Muhammad: "My earth and heaven cannot contain me, but the heart of my believing servant contains me." Merton comments: "The heart only is capable of knowing God." The heart is the only place strong enough to bear the divine secret; and the divine secret is that the Ground of being, which sustains all that is, is the Hidden Ground of Love. To know God as the Hidden Ground of Love is to *know that we are loved.* In *Contemplative Prayer,* Merton writes: "Our knowledge of God is paradoxically a knowledge *not of Him as the object of our scrutiny, but of ourselves as utterly dependent* on His saving and merciful knowledge of us" (*CPR,* 103–4). In a letter to a friend who confided to him her desire to love God more than everything that exists, Merton readily identifies with this desire; yet he adds: "Beyond all is a love of God in and through all that exists. We must not hold them apart one from another. But he must be One in all, and Is" (*HGL,* 346).

So, my friends, let us sing "How Great Thou Art," preferably in liturgy rather than into a shaving mirror. But remember that no words or images of ours can ever probe the meaning of God's greatness. Only love can know. Only the intimacy of love can experience. Or in Pascal's words: "The heart has its reasons which reason does not know."

CHAPTER THREE

The Presence of God

The only One Who can teach me to find God is God, Himself, Alone.

—Thomas Merton, *NSC*

In the last chapter I suggested that the question Who is God? does not admit of even a relatively satisfactory answer. The divine Reality transcends the ability of human language to capture that Reality in words. It will always remain a mystery, but a mystery that invites our continual reflection. Reflection, study, and prayer open tiny windows onto that divine Reality, though it always eludes our comprehension.

In this chapter let us try to deal with another question about God. Granted we cannot say in any adequate way who God is, but perhaps we can do a bit better on the question, Where do I find God? Or, to put the question even more simply, Where is God? For those readers who belong to the pre–Vatican II period in the life of the Roman Catholic Church, this question will surely send their memories scurrying back to that great museum piece of our past, the Baltimore catechism; and out of memory's deep recesses will come the answer indelibly impressed there: "God is everywhere."

"God is everywhere!" Let's pause a moment just to let the stupendous reality of that statement sink into our minds and hearts. Nothing can compare with such an impressive and moving statement. God is everywhere! Every time we say it or think about it, we ought to feel compelled to shout: Wow! Then we

might need some quiet time to recover from the full impact of that fantastic, fascinating truth. So important is it that we need to be continually reminded of it. Every day skywriters should write it in the air above us. Countless blimps, like the one that hovers over Super Bowls, should ride our skies, trailing signs with the wondrous message: "God is everywhere."

In April of 1994 I was invited to give the principal talk at a Spirituality Faire held in our diocese. The theme for that year was *God.* I was asked to talk about awareness of the presence of God. We tried to arrange that when I finished my talk, hundreds of balloons would float down from the ceiling carrying the message, God is everywhere! It would have been impressive, but at the last moment technology failed us and we were not able to do it.

I have thought seriously about writing a somewhat unique book which I would expect to become a best-seller. It would have one sentence on the first page. The sentence would be: "God is everywhere." This would be followed by two hundred blank pages. The readers would be advised to go through those pages slowly and carefully in order to allow the great truth on page 1 to sink deeply into their consciousness. So far I haven't located a publisher for this book. It would certainly be an easy book to write and a delightful one to read with care and attention over a period of several days; for it would take several days for an earnest reader to recover from experiencing so stupendous a truth.

Does anyone who "worked" the catechism in grade school remember having any such emotional reaction in encountering that question? I confess I didn't. I just went on to the next question, and it is not nearly so impressive as the previous one ought to have been. In fact, the next question destroys the mood that the first question should have created. For if you recall that little gray paperback book, you may remember that, following this marvelous answer to a great question, the catechism goes on to ask another question. Sad to say, it's the wrong question. It asks: "If God is everywhere, why do we not see Him?" The answer: "We cannot see God, because He is a

pure spirit and cannot be seen with bodily eyes" [or "goggily
eyes" as some of us cheerfully and unmaliciously read it].

The reason I say that we have here the wrong question and
answer is that they don't take us anywhere. We can't see God,
so the obvious reaction is "let's get on to another question." It's
a pity. Logically that second question should have been: "If
God is everywhere, how can we experience His presence? How
can we make that truth 'God is everywhere' an experience in
our lives? How can we enjoy the intimacy with God that this
statement so obviously implies?" Now those are questions that
really go somewhere. It is questions such as these that are at
the heart of any true spirituality. Answering them is the only
way of giving meaning to the life of prayer, to the contemplative experience. It is the only way of understanding intimacy
with God.

This magnificent statement: "God is everywhere" offers endless possibilities for fruitful reflection. What does the statement mean? What does it imply? Understanding what it means
and what it implies will help us see the way to that true intimacy with God which prayer is all about.

The Meaning of the Statement
"God Is Everywhere"

Before we speak about how we can experience God's presence, let us be clear about what it means to say that God is
everywhere. Simply put, it means is that *everywhere we are, we are
in the presence of God.* When we drive our cars, we are in the
presence of God. When we play golf or go to a ball game or
read a good book or eat a meal or take a drink—we are in the
presence of God. As we come together for a meal or a liturgy,
we are in the presence of God. God is everywhere. There are
no privileged places where God is more present than in others.
For God is fully and totally present wherever God is. There may
be places more conducive to prayer than others, such as a
church building or the solitude of your room or a quiet walk in

the woods. But this does not mean that God is more present in these places than in any other place. For God is fully and totally everywhere. Especially important for each of us is that God is always, in Augustine's felicitous phrase, *interior intimo meo,* "inside my most intimate self." (For a further clarification, see the concluding part of this chapter.)

An old song has it: "I want to go where you go, do what you do, love when you love—then, I'll be happy." This is the romantic statement of a lover wanting always to be one with the beloved; yet very early he or she has to realize that it's a desire that can never be fully achieved. There are times when the lover has to be absent from his or her beloved. But for us, being in the presence of God is not just a romantic desire. It is an ontological necessity. We have to "want to go" where God "goes," for there is literally nowhere else to go. To go where God is not would be quite literally to go into nothingness. It would mean, quite simply, to cease to be.

Let me try to clarify a bit more this wondrous truth that God is everywhere by reflecting on the fact that modern technology has made it possible for us to be in so many places. Because of the unprecedented advances in travel capabilities you and I can be anywhere. We can travel to Europe, to China, to Australia— you name it. *We can be anywhere we want, but we cannot be everywhere.* We cannot be *everywhere,* because our very nature as creatures requires that we be *somewhere.* That is to say, we have to be in some particular place that has limits and boundaries to it. Thus, if you take a trip to England, you can go *anywhere* in England, but, since you can only be in one place at a time, you always have to be *somewhere.* You can be in London and then in York. But because London and York are in different places (are different "somewheres"), you can only be in one or the other. You cannot be in both at the same time. *We always, I repeat, have to be somewhere, in some place that has limits.*

God, on the other hand, is *everywhere.* Now everywhere must not be thought of as a lot of "somewheres," as if you could say: "God sure is in a lot of places." No, "everywhere" transcends all "somewheres." There are no limits to God's presence. That is why, as I mentioned in the preceding chapter, God must not be thought of *as an object*. For an object—a building, a car, a woman, a man—is always *somewhere*, in some limited place. An object always takes up a certain amount of space. By its very nature an object cannot be everywhere. The fact that God is everywhere is the reason we must not think of God as an object. Most of the problems we have about God come from the mistake of thinking of God as an object, as a thing—as one thing alongside a lot of other things. Objects, things, persons take up space, because they are somewhere. God takes up no space; for God is everywhere, which is to say that God transcends space. He keeps in existence all the things that are in space.

> *No need to move*
> *Over that God may*
> *Have space.*
> *For God is*
> *Right there*
> *Sustaining all things,*
> *Each person and*
> *object in its*
> *Own proper place.*

Even when we say that God is in some particular place (which we see as part of "everywhere")—for instance, in the room where we are now—it is not the same as saying that a friend is sitting in a chair in the same room with you. It is true that you can make the statement: "God is present in the room," and the further statement "My friend is present in the room." But in each case you are talking about a very different kind of presence. You could be just as truly in that room if your friend were absent; or your friend could leave and you could say goodbye to her. Then you would no longer be in the presence of your friend, but you would be no less present in the room because she has departed it. Since your presence there does not depend on her presence, her departure has no effect on your continuing to be in the room. But think of you and God being in that room. If God were to leave the room, we would be saying good-bye not just to God but to our very selves. For apart from God's presence, we simply do not exist. God is the necessary and indispensable setting of my very being.

There is a fine hymn we sing regularly in our chapel. It is called "I Sing the Mighty Power of God." It has one super-fluous line that reads: "Everywhere that I may be, O God, be present there." This is not an object of prayer but a necessity of my being.

Implications of the Statement "God Is Everywhere"

The Presence of God as the Setting of Prayer

If God is everywhere, that means that *we are at all times in the situation, the setting, that makes prayer possible.* For we are at all times in the presence of the One whom we desire to touch, to reach, in prayer. We don't have to go looking for God, as if God were somehow missing from our lives.

One day two young boys, Joey and Mike, were walking down the street and passed a church. Joey said, "Jeez, Mike, I ain't been to confession in a long time. I think I'll go now." They entered the church. Joey went into the confessional. "I want to go to confession, Father," he said. The priest told him to begin his confession. It had been a long time. The lad finally admit-ted: "I don't know how to do it." The confessor, deciding this boy needed some instruction, began questioning him to see if he knew his catechism. So he asked: "Where is God?" The lad, bewildered, said: "Beg your pardon, Father?" The priest repeated his question more emphatically: "Where is God?" Thereupon the young boy jumped up, ran out of the confes-sional, grabbed his friend by the hand, rushing him out of the church: "Mike," he said in a trembling voice, "we gotta get out of here. God's missing and they think we've got him."

God isn't missing. We don't have to search for God. We don't have to find God. It is not that God is *there* and we are *here*. Rather, God is there and here and everywhere. We are, as I say, *always in the setting or situation of prayer.* We might express it this way: God is always in touch with us, because we are always in God's saving presence. But we are not always in touch with God, because so often we are forgetful of the Presence of God.

God's Presence as the Necessary Condition of Our Existence

Being in the presence of God is not only the setting in which we work and pray, it is the *necessary condition of our existence* and of the existence of everything that is. When we say God is "everywhere," we don't mean that God is *just there* in a static sort of way. No, God is—if I may put it this way—effortlessly busy everywhere. God is the *Source* of my being and the *Ground* of Love; God enables me to continue in being. And this is true of everyone and everything that exists. God is making me *be.* God is making me *act.* God is making me *be* and *act freely.* The paradox of God's making me act *freely* is one that I will not go into now. But suffice it to say that being in the presence of God is not something I choose, as if I were to say: "I guess I'll spend some time in the presence of God today." Or, "I'm going on retreat next week; I'll be able to spend a lot of time in the presence of God." No, being in God's presence is not a matter of choice. It is not, for example, like saying: "I think I will go visit my friend who is in the hospital." Being in the presence of God is an ontological necessity. The salesman for the American Express checks says: "Don't leave home without them." But we can, if we so choose. We can't, however, go anywhere without God. For "anywhere without God" is simply the realm of non-existence; it is quite literally nowhere. What a grand relief it is for us to know that we are *somewhere* and that God is *everywhere.*

Where is God?
I don't know.

I haven't got Him [Her].
Oh, yes, you have!

God's Presence as the Basis
for the Essential Oneness of All Reality

Yet another implication that follows from the fact that God is everywhere is the *essential oneness of all reality*. While I am distinct from God (in the sense that I obviously am not God), still I am not separate from God, for apart from God (separate from God), I would simply cease to be. But this is true not just of me; it is true of every person and everything that is. *Everything that is, is in God. It cannot be apart from God.* If this is true, then it follows that, since I am one with God and you are one with God, we are one with each other. We are one with all reality.

It would be well to state at this point that we are one with God and with one another in our *being*. But in our *existences* creatures differ from one another. Each created being exists in a unique set of circumstances proper to itself. Thus, each human being, as we have already pointed out, is always somewhere, is limited to a particular time and place. (God, however, has no such limitations: being and existence are one and the same in God. God is everywhere.) Since we are distinct and different from one another in our existences, conflicts and violence may arise. Existence tends to divide. Being tends to unite. That is why contemplation, which puts us in touch with our deepest being and therefore with our universal oneness, is the principal basis for nonviolent love. Recognizing our oneness in being, despite the conflicts that different existences may engender, is the only way to true and lasting peace.

Intimacy with God

I tried to think of an appropriate term to sum up the meaning of this closeness we have with God and in God with one another and with all of reality. The term that came to me was ontological intimacy. Maybe that doesn't grab you at first. But let me explain what I mean by it. I mean intimacy at the level of being itself. Ontological intimacy with God is the necessary condition of everyone and indeed everything that exists. It has important implications for our relationship with God and also with other people. In touching them we touch God, from whom they come and in whom they are. The meaning of this intimacy is worth exploring.

Some time ago, I had occasion to do such an exploration. I was invited by one of our local parishes to be one of several speakers in a series they had planned for Lent. The general topic of the series was "intimacy," as experienced in different relationships, and I was asked to discuss our relationship of intimacy with God. In getting ready for this talk, I had to ask, What are we dealing with in these talks? What do we mean by intimacy? The best I could come up with on first reflection was that intimacy has a great deal to do with sharing, communication, and ultimately communion. It has to be a profound experience, which involves relating to another not just on the surface but in the inmost recesses of one's own being and that of the other.

What proved a very enlightening entry into the meaning of "intimacy" was a check of the dictionary. The word's etymology is quite fascinating. It takes its origin from the Latin word *intimus.* Now *intimus,* which is an adjective, derives, strangely, from an adverb, *intus,* which means "inside." Its comparative degree is *interior,* meaning "more inside"; its superlative, *intimus,* would mean "most inside." Intimacy, therefore, means people getting inside each other as deeply as possible.

In the wake of this discovery, I realized that, in the handing out of topics for the Lenten seminars, I got the better deal by far. I had been asked to talk about *intimacy with God.* The other speakers were to address various aspects of *human intimacy,* which meant that they had to discuss what people had to do to *create* intimacy. I had no such problem to deal with because intimacy with God is a unique kind of intimacy: we don't have to create it. It exists from the very moment we begin to exist. *To be created means to enter into intimacy with God.* It is not, therefore, something we have to bring into being. Rather, it is something we have to discover, but the point is that it is there for the discovering. That might be a helpful approach to contemplative prayer: thinking of it as the discovery of my intimacy with God.

Perhaps no one has described divine intimacy more felicitously than St. Augustine in his remarkable prayer to God in book 3 of the *Confessions,* where he says to God: "You are *interior intimo meo.*" Note how he uses both the comparative and the superlative of *intus.* The words have a profundity to them that is difficult to translate. "You are more inward to me than my most inward reality. . . . You are inside what is the most intimate part of me. . . . When I discover my most intimate self, I discover you there. . . . You are the interior of my interior. . . . When I get to my deepest depths, I shall find You." These are different ways of struggling to translate Augustine's *interior intimo meo.* It is like saying: "There is in me a place (which is really not a place) where I am most deeply and fully myself. This is my true self. If I find that most inward reality in myself, I will come to realize that, inseparable from that reality, yet deeper still than it, is God." In *New Seeds of Contemplation,* Thomas Merton speaks of "entering into the deepest center of [oneself] and [passing] through that center into God" (p. 64). This is what he meant when he spoke of God as the "Hidden Ground of Love" that is at the root of all reality. Augustine's words are movingly poetic—and they express a wonderful way into an understanding of prayer. Prayer is experiencing intimacy with God.

CHAPTER FOUR

Awareness of God's Presence

¶

Contemplation is a sudden gift of awareness, an awakening
to the Real within all that is real.

—Thomas Merton, *NSC*

Prayer gives joy to the spirit, peace to the heart. I speak of
prayer, not words. It is the longing for God, too deep for
words.

—St. John Chrysostom

Consider the following scenario. A wife and husband are sitting in their living room. She is knitting; he is devouring the sports page of the paper. All at once she says to him with quiet sarcasm: "You can stop saying 'Yes, dear,' every five minutes. I stopped talking to you a half hour ago."

The story describes a breakdown of communication and probably an unhealthy relationship: a husband talking perfunctorily to his wife, yet not really aware of her presence. Suppose we read the parable in the light of our relationship with God. We are always in the presence of God, yet we can pray to God in a distracted, perfunctory way, without really being aware of God's presence.

Now the husband in our story could go on saying "Yes, dear," even after his wife has gotten up and left the room. Nothing much would change except that she wouldn't be there. The situation would be quite different with us, if we were talking to God and all at once God decided to leave. Since the presence of God is the necessary condition of our very existence, we could not, if God were to leave us, go on mechanically saying our prayers. For if God removed the divine presence from us, we would simply cease to be.

We cannot *be* without the presence of God. But we can be without *being aware* of God's presence. Yet to live without awareness of God is to live in a world of illusion. It is to be out of touch with the real world. For the Great Fact of our lives is that we are always in the presence of God.

Let me make this very concrete by saying: *Each of us right now is as fully present in God as we shall ever be.* Even in heaven we will not be any more fully in the presence of God than we are at this moment. What heaven, the beatific vision, will mean is not that God will become more fully present to us (I repeat: God is *always* as fully present to us as possible). Rather, what heaven will mean is a change in our awareness of God's presence. *Heaven will mean that we shall be fully aware that we are in God's presence.* We need to do some revisions of our notion of heaven. It isn't really a kind of Hawaiian intercontinental hotel that is first empty and then begins to fill up as guests arrive who have the proper reservations. Actually, heaven isn't a place we go to. It is, quite simply, becoming ourselves fully and totally. This will happen not when God becomes more fully present to us but when we are *always fully aware* that we are in God's presence.

If you look at Thomas Merton's description of contemplation in the first chapter of *New Seeds of Contemplation,* you will discover that that is precisely the way in which he defines contemplation: as full awareness of the divine presence.

> Contemplation is the highest expression of man's intellectual and spiritual life. It is that life itself, fully active, *fully aware* that it is alive. . . . It is a *vivid realization* of the fact that life and being in us proceed from an invisible, transcendent and infinitely abundant Source. *Contemplation is, above all, awareness of that Source. . . . Contemplation is a sudden gift of awareness,* an awakening to the Real in all that is real. A vivid *awareness* of our contingent reality as received, as a present from God, as a free gift of love.

Is contemplation, then, something like the Emerald Isle, "a little bit of heaven"? Almost, but not quite. For this side of the eschatological divide, we experience the presence of God by faith, not by a face-to-face vision. Yet I hasten to add that contemplation is faith experienced at a deeper level and at a level of more profound consciousness. Normally we think of faith as grasping God through words, ideas, and symbols. The contemplative knows with a certitude that goes beyond images and words and concepts. It is thus a cut above what we ordinarily think of as faith-knowledge. In Merton's words, "Contemplation is always beyond our knowledge, beyond our own light, beyond systems, beyond explanations, beyond discourse, beyond dialogue." It is knowing "beyond all knowing or unknowing" (*NSC*, 2). Still, contemplation remains faith, not vision.

Also it must be said that the experience of God in contemplation is a free gift of God that comes when God chooses to give it. Hence it is not a constant in our lives. Still it is the closest we can come to heaven in this life. It is the moment when we are fully alive, fully awakened to the Real in all that is real and, therefore, fully in love with all that is.

Methods of Prayer?

Are there any ways of prayer that will help us to this deeper awareness of God's presence? If we look to Thomas Merton, we find that, when he was master of novices at Gethsemani, he did not go in for methods of prayer. He was content to let his novices find the way that was best for them, encouraging them not to say a lot of words but simply to be quietly and silently in God's presence. He would, of course, have introduced them to *lectio divina,* but would have invited them to use it with utmost freedom. They were not to get themselves confused on this "ladder" of prayer. He especially discouraged them from spending too much time in discursive thinking. I offer a strong *bravo* to that. I spent a long time in my life believing that mental prayer (which I saw as the only kind of prayer that differed from vocal prayer) required a good bit of reasoning in which I should come up with all sorts of wonderful insights about God.

Of course it didn't happen. It took me a long time to realize that quiet prayer did not require a lot of thinking about God.

To those who felt as I had, that a good deal of discursive reasoning was an essential of true prayer, Merton wrote:

> Those who have progressed a certain distance in the interior life not only *do not need to make systematic meditations, but rather profit by abandoning them* in favor of a simple and peaceful affective prayer, without fuss, without noise, without much speech, and with no more than one or two favorite ideas or mysteries, to which they return in a more or less general and indistinct manner each time they pray.
>
> The main thing is to establish contact with God by loving faith. This implies at least enough awareness for the mind to be alive in the Presence of God. (*WTW,* 95)

One thing must be made clear: Awareness of God must be precisely that—awareness of God. My attention must be centered on God, not on myself. I should not be watching myself pray to see if I am being aware of God. For when I do this I am being more aware of myself (being aware of God) than I am of God. A musician who is conscious of herself singing will probably not sing well. For she will be thinking of herself singing instead of losing herself in the music. If I think of God as an object which I as a subject am being aware of, then I have set myself apart from God. My awareness must be simple awareness or, if you will, simple awareness of God. But "I" as a subject of awareness must disappear. For the "I" that conceives itself as the *subject* of the contemplative experience is the false self that, as Merton says, is destined to disappear like smoke up a chimney. It is my true self that is in God.

If, in this context, you want a "tough" but brilliant Merton passage to reflect on, you might try this:

> [T]he experience of contemplation is the experience of God's life and presence within ourselves not as object but as the transcendent source of our own subjectivity. Contemplation is a mystery in which God reveals Himself to us as the very center of our own most intimate self—*intimior* [*sic:* Augustine used "*interior*"] *intimo meo* as St. Augustine said. When the realization of His

presence bursts upon us, our own self disappears in Him and we pass mystically through the Red Sea of separation to lose ourselves (and thus find our true selves) in Him. (*NM*, 19)

That's a paragraph worth rereading! In reality it's about the gospel paradox that to find ourselves we have to lose ourselves. True self-identity comes, paradoxically, through *apparent* self-annihilation.

Difference: Thinking and Being Aware

Still another clarification about awareness. *It is not a synonym for thinking.* There is a big difference between *thinking* about the presence of God and *being aware* of that presence. Thinking about God makes God into an object and hence creates the dichotomy of a subject relating to an object, leading us into dualism. Awareness, on the other hand, transcends that dichotomy, as our subjectivity becomes one with the subjectivity of God.

There is, as it were, nothing between us, nothing to separate us from God. We are not aware of God as something, we are *simply aware.* Let me offer a couple of simple analogies that may prove helpful. Suppose you see a beautiful red rose. You can *think* about that rose if you choose. That means that you as a subject examine the rose and its characteristics as an object. You notice it has a green stem, some leaves, lovely red petals. You can count the number of petals. You could go farther and examine the rose in a laboratory. Notice what you are doing. You are putting distance between yourself and the rose. You a subject are analyzing it as an object. But suppose that, instead of thinking about the rose in this discursive way, you *simply look* at it and let yourself be drawn into the beauty of color, the fragrance of odor, the comeliness of shape. The more you look at it and let yourself become absorbed in it, the more you forget about yourself. There is no longer subject-object. You enter into a state of intimacy. You become one with the rose. In a sense you as a separate subject are no longer there.

This understanding that awareness is not thinking is most important to the contemplative experience. Fr. Hugo Enomiya-Lassale, who teaches spirituality at Sophia University in Tokyo, says: "My most difficult task is to teach people *not to think!*"

Here is another example that will illustrate the difference between "thinking" and "being aware." Several years ago, I was at the National Gallery in London. At the time they had a special display of Leonardo da Vinci's marvelous drawing (unfinished) of "The Virgin and Child with St. Anne [Elizabeth somehow got left out of the drawing] and St. John the Baptist." It was in a small room all by itself; there was a bench in the center of the room where one could sit quietly and look. For about half an hour I sat there, all alone, powerfully moved by this masterpiece. Now during that time, I could have thought about that drawing and analyzed what made it a masterpiece. I could have noted the peculiar darkness in St. Anne's eyes and compared that to the light in Mary's. I could have looked at the child of St. Elizabeth and noted how his eyes were fixed on Jesus. I could have looked into the face of Jesus and seen the pensive, reflective look on his face. I would, in doing all these things, be thinking about the drawing. Notice how the thinking separates me from the drawing. I am a subject analyzing an object. The more I think of it the more distance I place between it and myself. But suppose that, instead of thinking about it, I simply sat there in awe, allowing myself to be drawn into the beauty before me. Totally forgetful of myself, I could let the drawing's beauty become so identified with me that I would become one with the drawing. As Merton expressed it somewhat whimsically in the draft of a poem written on 18 February 1965 (in a writing notebook he sent to the University of Syracuse):

> The main thing is knowing how to see,
> To see without starting to think,
> To see when you see
> And not to think when you see . . .

The Prayer of Awareness
and Other Forms of Prayer

Awareness of God's presence, which is at the heart of contemplative and of wordless prayer is what gives meaning to all forms of prayer. Think of the vocal prayers we say. Awareness of God's presence should accompany all our vocal prayer, whether personal or liturgical. Our private vocal prayers, our praying liturgy, our participation in Eucharist or Baptism or Reconciliation or Marriage take on a special depth, if we pray with this awareness of the divine Presence. It will make us realize that when we pray we are never alone. Being aware that we are in the presence of God means being aware of our oneness with one another and with all of God's good creation. When we praise God and thank God, it is always with the awareness that we are totally dependent on God and that we are in God. When we pray for reconciliation, we are aware of our failure to live out all that intimacy which God requires of us. When we offer intercession, it is with the awareness of our radical need for God, since we are totally dependent on God for our existence and for our continued existence.

Whereas vocal prayer is, in one way or another, an expression of our dependence on God, wordless prayer or prayer of awareness—that time of attentiveness to God's presence—is more aptly described as an *experience of that dependence*. At the same time, it is an experience of our intimacy with God and our oneness with all that is.

I would like to invite you to daily practice of the "prayer of awareness." It doesn't require *doing* anything special. It simply means spending time *just being* in the presence of God in silence and wordlessness, though one need not be too much of a purist: we may need an occasional word to help preserve our attentiveness. One happy thing about this approach to prayer: you don't have to get anywhere. For you are already and always there: in the presence of God. You are just wanting to be more attentive and more lovingly responsive to that presence. "Not getting anywhere" may seem discouraging and could tempt one to give up the practice of "prayer of awareness." But I guarantee that such prayer, daily adhered to, will do things to us. It will deepen our sense of who we are. It will make us more loving, more considerate, more compassionate toward our sisters and brothers. For sooner or later our awareness of God's presence leads us to awareness of our inner self and to awareness of God's people. It creates in us both a sense of our own identity and a social consciousness.

Awareness of God Leads to Awareness of Our Own Identity

Some time ago a young couple who are friends of mine decided they would go on sabbatical for a year in southwestern United States. Sally was a writer and Jim a school teacher. They had been able to save enough money to make the sabbatical possible and were looking forward to it with joy. Sally told me that during the sabbatical she hoped to engage in some reflection, some praying and, because she is a writer, to try to finish a book she had been working on for some time.

Two or three months went by. One day I received a rather despondent letter from Sally, saying that she seemed to be getting nowhere in her writing and was quite discouraged about it. I wrote reminding her that she had gone on this sabbatical to have time for rest, reflection, and praying. I said, further, that I thought she should not let herself get caught up in the production-oriented mentality of our society and think that her sabbatical would be a failure if she did not "produce something." I suggested to her that it was enough for her simply to "be" during her sabbatical. There really wasn't anything she *had* to do.

She wrote back and thanked me for sharing these reflections and said: "Now when people ask me what I *do*, I simply tell that I am a human *being*."

We all have to learn that we must be, each of us, a human *being* and not just a human *doing*. We have to discover ever more deeply the value of silence and quiet and solitude. We

need to have, in the words of the title of one of Paul Tillich's
books: "The Courage [just] to Be." We need to get over the fear
we sometimes have that "we are doing nothing" or that we have
"nothing to do." Isn't it odd that so many of us are quite accom-
plished in wasting time but aren't at all good at "doing nothing." By that I mean "doing nothing and just being." It is only in
being (which calls for some kind of quiet and a relaxed atmosphere) that we can come to know who we are. If we are only "*do-
ers,*" and never "*be-ers,*" we shall never really know who it is that
is doing what we do. We shall be strangers to ourselves. And
strangers to God too; for our being is the "place" of our union
with God.

> *To be*
> *Or not to be?*
> *That was*
> *Hamlet's question. Ours is:*
> *Is to do*
> *the only way*
> *To be?*

Unfortunately, our culture does not encourage us to find joy
and contentment in times when we are able just to be. Thomas
Merton more than once reminded his readers that in a culture
that makes us believe that every minute has to be put to some
useful purpose, we have to learn the value of the useless. Read
his sparkling essay "Rain and the Rhinoceros," in *Raids on the
Unspeakable.* Here is a brief, teasing sampling:

> One who is not alone has not discovered his identity. He seems
> to be alone, perhaps, for he experiences himself as "individual."
> But because he is willingly enclosed and limited by the laws and
> illusions of collective existence, he has no more identity than an
> unborn child in the womb. He is not yet conscious. He is alien to
> his own truth. He has life, but no identity. To have an identity he
> has to be awake and aware . . . of the invulnerable inner reality
> which we cannot recognize (which we can only *be*), but to which
> we awaken only when we see the unreality of our vulnerable
> shell. The discovery of this inner self is an act and affirmation of
> solitude. (pp. 14–15)

That "invulnerable inner reality," that "inner self" is our identity. To discover it we have need of some solitude (see chapter 5), in which we can become experts at doing nothing and just being. This calls for a good bit of letting go. We must, for some moments in our lives, let go of the things that are in our minds and hearts: our thoughts, our plans, our desires, our concerns, our anxieties. Putting them aside for a time does not mean that we do not have to deal with them at the proper time. But there must be those moments when, for the while at least, we let go of them (so that later we can deal with them afresh).

This "letting go" is difficult. For our minds are going all the time—like a watch I used to have that was kept going simply by the motion of the hand without ever having to be wound up. We don't have to be wound up either: we are so deluged with thoughts, feelings, and concerns that we are scarcely aware of their diversity, or sometimes even of their presence. They fragment us and scatter our energies. They hide our inner unity. They prevent us, therefore, from knowing who we are.

Yet fearfully we hang on to our activities, because somehow we feel that letting go of them poses a threat to our very identity. Descartes' dictum "*Cogito, ergo sum*" ("I think, therefore I am"), which has so strongly influenced Western thought since the seventeenth century, is translated into *Ago, ergo sum* ("I act, therefore I am"). This is to say that I am sure that *I am* precisely because I *do something*, whether that something be seeing, speaking, thinking, or some other type of activity. So we tend to look upon our walking, our conversations, our producing something as if they constituted our personal identity. Apart from them, we seem scarcely to exist.

We need to learn that just being, without doing anything, is a fruitful, even necessary, form of prayer. It is at the heart of the "prayer of awareness" that I am recommending. Thomas Merton wrote to Sister Therese Lentfoehr, who had asked him about prayer:

> About prayer: have you a garden or somewhere that you can walk in, by yourself? Take half an hour or fifteen minutes a day and just walk up and down among the flowerbeds. . . . Do not try to

think about anything in particular and when thoughts about
work, etc. come to you, do not try to push them out by main
force, but see if you can't drop them just by relaxing your mind.
Do this because you are "praying." . . . But if thoughts about
work will not go away, accept them idly and without too much
eagerness, with the intention of letting God reveal His will to you
through these thoughts. (*RJ,* 195)

As I have already mentioned, spending time "just being"
does not by any means dispense us from the activities that our
life situation calls us to carry out. We are not allowed to shirk
the responsibilities that are ours: the things that we must do to
live our own lives fully and to be attentive to the needs of our
sisters and brothers. But the time of letting go in prayer will
help us to keep things in balance so that our daily activities do
not overwhelm us and fragment our inner unity.

Time spent in "just being" will give us a new sense of who we
are. It will strengthen us to do better whatever it is we have to
do. For *we* will really *be* there in the doing. Once we have discovered our identity in God, we will have more accurate insight
into life and the priorities we need to set for ourselves. We may
come to learn that we are now able to take in stride many of the
things that once unsettled us. Our inner unity will give us a
consciousness of authentic freedom. We shall be enabled to
stand on our own feet and make decisions of conscience that
are our own and not vicarious decisions made for us by someone else. Like the lady from Tucson, whom I mentioned in
chapter 1, we have permission, *from our own spirit,* to continue
our journey toward wholeness of life. I hasten to add that I have
no intention of suggesting that being able to respond to our
own inner truth in freedom makes authority in community
unimportant or even unnecessary. Freedom and authority are
not incompatible. Authority properly exercised can offer
authentic guidelines that can help me respond to my inner
truth. Since freedom is exercised in community, where my
decisions must interact with the decisions of other people,
authority can be helpful in clarifying the concrete ways in
which this interaction of decisions can serve and promote the

common good of all. Thus, authority, when it respects my inner truth, can enhance my freedom: for it helps me to exercise it wisely.

On the other hand, freedom is not compatible with authoritarianism. Authoritarianism is authority acting with naked power. Authority degenerates into authoritarianism when it imposes its dictates without dialogue and without regard for the inner truth of the subjects of that authority. One expects to find authoritarianism in institutions that are totalitarian in character. It is surely surprising—though unfortunately not an uncommon experience—to find it in institutions that should by their very nature be committed to fostering and preserving freedom. Much of Thomas Merton's writings in his later years shows a deep concern to unmask elements of unfreedom existing in American society and also in the church.

Tyger, Tyger, Burning Bright . . .

There is an oft-told Hindu story about the tiger and the sheep. Once upon a time there was a flock of sheep grazing peacefully in the fields. A female tiger chanced upon them. She happened to be pregnant, but still her tiger instincts moved her to attack the sheep. In the course of her leap, she gave birth to a baby tiger but died in the process.

The sheep, seeing the dead tiger, finally had the courage to return. They discovered the baby tiger and, pitying this poor orphan, adopted him. The "teachers" in the flock taught him how to bleat and how to chew grass. He was a slow learner but eventually mastered it and discovered what he thought was his identity, namely, being a sheep.

One day the sheep were in a field again, grazing. Along came another tiger. He attacked the sheep and they all scurried away—all, that is, but the little tiger. He just stood there almost casually. He wasn't afraid at all. In fact he looked up at the big tiger—and bleated at him. The big tiger was disgusted with such conduct. He grabbed the little tiger by the ear and took him to a pool of water and had him look in and see that he was the image and likeness of the big tiger. But the little tiger didn't get it. So the big tiger took him to his cave, where he had the remains of a deer he had killed the day before. He tried to get the little tiger to eat some of the flesh, but the little fellow turned away, nauseated by the sight. Finally, in desperation the big one opened the mouth of the little one and forced some of the meat into his mouth. The little tiger tasted the blood running down his throat and began to chew. Then suddenly everything was changed—and he let out the roar of a tiger! All his life he had mistaken his identity: his "culture" made him think he was a sheep. He never took the time to discover who he really was. Now in this moment in the cave he discovered at last that he was no sheep but a tiger. He found his true identity.

The prayer of awareness, wordless prayer, the prayer of "just being," is our going into the cave to discover and rediscover ever more fully our true identity. Unless we find regular times in our lives simply to be, our "doing" will chop us to bits. It will so compartmentalize our lives that we may never come to know who we are. We will live our lives as bleating tigers eating grass.

Awareness of God Leads to Awareness of Our Sisters and Brothers

In December 1966, John Hunt, senior editor of the *Saturday Evening Post,* wrote to Thomas Merton inviting him to write an article on monasticism for that journal's "Speaking Out" column. Merton was interested but had his own ideas about what he should say to the readers of the *Post.* He proposed an article with the title "Speaking Out for the Inside." The point of the article would be to help people realize that life does have an interior dimension of depth and awareness. The unfortunate predicament of so many people is that this interiority is blocked out by a life that concentrates on externals.

The plight of these people [this is Shannon speaking, not Merton] might be likened to that of the people of Europe before the discovery of the New World. The only world they knew was Europe; and all the while there was a whole other world, full of new and marvelous things of which they knew nothing. That world was there, but they were unaware. Once they discovered it, all sorts of new adventures became possible.

In a somewhat similar way people who know only the externals of life are cut off from a realm of their own reality that offers new and exciting experiences that far surpass the kind of life that is possible at the level of just the superficial.

In the course of clarifying what he would write about [I am back to Merton again, though I should say that the article he intended was never actually written or, if it was written, it was never published], Merton says to Hunt: "The inner life and freedom of man begins when this inner dimension opens up and man lives *in communion with the unknown within himself.* On the basis of this he can also be *in communion with the same unknown in others*" (*WTF,* 329-30)

Perceptive readers may recall that these words are similar to Merton's words quoted earlier (in chapter 2), where he describes prayer to his novices as "entering into the unknown." In his writings on spirituality Merton is constantly pointing to the existence of this marvelous interior life in all of us. When we miss it, we miss most of what is truly real in us.

To speak of this divine presence in us is simply to particularize the general theme running through this book, namely, "that God is everywhere." Yet it is only when we begin to experience God in the depths of our own being that this wondrous truth, "God is everywhere," ceases to be merely an article of faith we believe in or a conclusion of reason we assent to and becomes a reality of personal experience. It becomes what Merton calls a "communion with the Unknown" within us.

But this is only a beginning. Our inner life does not exist in isolation. It is linked with the inner life of everyone else. How can I say that? Because the "Unknown" whom we meet in our depths is the same "Unknown" who dwells in the depths of all of God's people. This is why Merton can say "communion with the Unknown" in ourselves becomes the basis for "communion with that same Unknown in others." I wish there were some way I could make these words leap off the page and really grab you and me and all of humanity. They are awe-inspiring! What they say to me is that in experiencing God in the depths of my being, I also experience each and every one of you, because you also are in communion with God. In God we are truly one with one another. I am one with each and everyone of you and all of you with me.

Let me make this very concrete. Suppose you are at a shopping mall. You watch people milling about, going in and out of various stores. As you see them on the surface of reality, they seem to be all separate from one another. Yet if you move to a deeper level on consciousness—that level wherein alone you see reality as it really is, wherein alone you meet the "Unknown" in yourselves as the same "Unknown" who is in these "others"— you are able to let go of the "illusion" of separateness. You are able to see that you and they are all one.

It was rather sneaky of me to write the above paragraph. For I was really describing an actual experience that Thomas Merton had. On 18 March 1958 he had gone into Louisville to see about the printing of a new postulants' guide. Standing at the corner of Fourth and Walnut Streets, he had a deep experience of interiority. He saw people going in and coming out of stores in a shopping district (there weren't any malls then). All at once he was overwhelmed with the realization that he loved these people and that they belonged to him as he belonged to them. He was snapped forever out of the illusion of thinking that because he lived in a monastery and followed an ancient rule that he was somehow separate from them. He was energized by the joy of simply being a human person and being united with, not separated from, the rest of the human race.

Later as he reflected on the experience and wrote about it, he was moved by the splendor of it all:

> Then it was as if I suddenly saw the secret beauty of their hearts, the depths of their hearts, where neither sin nor desire nor self-knowledge can reach, the core of their being, the person that each one is in God's eyes. If only they could see themselves as

they really are. If only we could see each other that way all the time. There would be no more war, no more hatred, no more greed. (*CGB*, 158)

This experience awakened in Merton a sense of responsibility to his fellow men and women and moved him to involvement, through his writings, in the great social issues of his day. So too for us: as soon as we let go of the notion of separateness, we know that we are responsible for one another, especially for those who are in need. My responsibilities to the homeless, the sick, the needy, the oppressed, the marginalized spring from that deep oneness in God that I have with them and with all my sisters and brothers. I must love them as myself, for in a very real way they are "my other self." As Thomas Merton said in Calcutta in a gathering of people from many religious traditions: "We are already one. But we imagine that we are not. And what we have to recover is our original unity. What we have to be is what we are" (*AJ*, 308).

The equation of Christian social responsibility is this: coming to know God in our own inner selves means coming to know people, and coming to know people means getting involved with them and with their problems. And that involvement takes place in history, in the here-and-now of their lifetime and ours. In a 1966 article in *Commonweal*, Merton articulated a "ministry" insight that grew out of his contemplative experience: "That I should have been born in 1915, that I should be the contemporary of Auschwitz, Hiroshima and the Watts riots are things about which I was not first consulted. Yet they are also events in which, whether I like it or not, *I am deeply and personally involved*" (*CWA*, 161).

And what of ourselves? If we have really become aware of our oneness with all our sisters and brothers, dare we be uninvolved in the predicaments that belong to their history and ours? How we become involved in particular areas of responsibility (especially those that deal with violence and conflict) is a topic we shall discuss later. But what calls us to this involvement is what this chapter is all about.

I read recently, in a book whose author and title I cannot

remember, the story of a father and his ten-year-old daughter who were watching the news on TV, as they ate their dessert. At one point in the news, a South African black man was forced out of his home by a group of youthful thugs. They followed him, pelting him with stones and finally stoning him to death. The little girl was quiet; then she asked: "Daddy, did this really happen or is this just make-believe on a TV show?" Somewhat uncomfortably, the father told her it was real. Her next question made him even more uncomfortable: "Daddy, why didn't the man with the camera help the person who was killed by the stones?"

This young girl's simple question evokes several other questions. Do the camera person and the other media people cease to be members of the human community when they are out seeking "an objective picture" of the news? Does their role relieve them of all human responsibility to those whose story they are telling? Are they simply innocent bystanders watching a crime unfold, with a concern just to tell the story, but with no concern to involve themselves in the story?

Must we not say, not just about media people but about ourselves, that those who see violence, injustice, and dehumanizing actions lose their innocence if they fail to act and do what they can. They become guilty bystanders.

If someone asks, Where can we begin? perhaps the simplest answer is: Right where you are. Start with the people you rub elbows with every day. See them in God and as one with you in God. If everyone who reads this chapter were to do that and if each of them got another person to do the same, pockets of peace and harmony would spring up in many places, as people found in one another the Unknown who is source of being and ground of love for us all. This would be an effective way of sowing seeds of peace.

Forgetfulness of the Presence of God

If the Great Fact of our lives is that we are always in the presence of God, the Great Problem of our lives is that we are so often unaware of God's presence. The great joy of contemplative prayer is that God never forgets us (i.e., God always keeps us in existence); the anguish the contemplative must live with is the sad realization that the sense of our intimacy with God is continually slipping from our memory. We are like the seven-year-old girl who in her Christmas letter to God wrote: "I'm sorry I haven't been praying lately. I will from now on. Amen." Like her, we make this resolution too. But forgetfulness is so quick to return.

It should be clear that forgetfulness of the presence of God is not like ordinary forgetfulness, such as forgetting where you put your car keys or forgetting someone's birthday. The first may curtail your driving for the time being, and the second may put you in someone's bad graces. But *forgetting about the presence of God and the intimacy with God that it engenders is forgetting about the setting and context of all reality*. It is forgetting what is essential to my very being and to that of everything that exists. It is forgetting what is truly real.

But we are so prone to forgetfulness. We can be forgetful of God even when we pray, as when we pray to a God who is distant from us rather than to the God in whom we are, in whom we live and move and have our being. Forgetting the presence of God can have repercussions on our relationships with our sisters and brothers and all of the world. For it can lead us to ignore the sacredness and dignity of every person and indeed of every thing that God has made. For we and they are all one in God. But when we forget the presence of God, we forget this fundamental oneness. We see others as separate, not as they really are—one with us and one with one another, because all are one in God. To be aware of the presence of God and the intimacy with God which that presence makes possible is also to understand the deepest roots of any sort of human intimacy. God is the interior of my interior, but God is also the interior of all of us. We all meet in God. This makes for the deepest possible intimacy. To forget the presence of God and the oneness of all reality which it implies is to forget what makes human intimacy possible, at least human intimacy in its most profound meaning.

Forgetfulness: A Corporate Experience of Humanity

This forgetfulness of our oneness with God is not just a personal experience, it is the corporate experience of humanity. Indeed, this is one way of understanding original sin. *We are in God, but we don't seem to know it. We are in paradise, but we don't realize it.* The mythical picture of the paradisiacal state described in Genesis suggests a marvelous intimacy of the man and the woman with God, as they walked with God in the cool of the evening. They were one too with the rest of reality. For harmony and peace were everywhere.

Forgetfulness as Original Sin

The "fall" must not be viewed as a historical event, in which Adam and Eve eat the apple and the rest of us get the stomachache. No, the "fall" is a fall from the oneness and harmony of paradise into disunity, alienation, and a sense of separation. It is the loss of divine intimacy—and human intimacy too. Humanity has fallen not into the real world but into a world of illusions and unreality. We no longer see things as they truly are. Where there is oneness, we see separateness; where there is harmony, we see alienation and manipulation of people. It is not so much that this oneness is taken away. It is present in us, hidden in the depths of our being, but it lies there forgotten.

A Way of Understanding Redemption

What Jesus does in redeeming us is to wake us from the death-like sleep of separateness. Is this not the point of that striking liturgical hymn that Paul quotes in Ephesians 5:14?

> Sleeper, awake!
> Rise from the dead
> And Christ will shine on you. (NRSV)

He rouses us from the forgetfulness of unity, so that we recover what was always there. We didn't know it was there because we had forgotten. If you shine a bright light on a person who is asleep, most likely they will wake up. As the beautiful *Exultet*, the Easter hymn in honor of the "Light of Christ," says: "Christ the Morning Star, come back from the dead, sheds his peaceful light on all humankind." And we wake from our sleep of forgetfulness.

CHAPTER FIVE

Silence, Solitude, Quiet Time

The hen does not lay eggs in the marketplace.
—A Sufi saying

The door to solitude opens only from the inside.
—Thomas Merton, *DQ*

"The only way to live [is] to live in a world that [is] charged with the presence and reality of God" (*Seven Storey Mountain*, 191). This was the conclusion Thomas Merton came to, he tells us in *The Seven Storey Mountain*, during the summer of 1938, when he was reading William Blake in preparation for writing his thesis for his master's degree. He admitted, however, that at that time this realization was more of an intellectual understanding than a reality he was actually experiencing in his life.

This is the problem we all have to deal with, isn't it? You and I can accept everything I have said up to now about the presence of God and the implications of that presence; but it may be an acceptance that grips our minds only. It sounds great! Let the skywriters blazon across the heavens: "God is everywhere!" Let balloons fall all about us with that wondrous message! But if it is to be more than a kind of intellectual euphoria, if it is to have meaning in our daily living, we need to transfer it from the mind to the heart, from the realm of intellectual knowledge to that of lived experience.

And let us be honest and realistic about this. It is by no means an easy task. Indeed, it is almost impossible for us, if we are overbusy, if our lives are frantic, distraught, and overwhelmed with too much activity. And "frantic," "distraught," "overwhelmed" are probably adjectives that fit the lives of most of us.

Quiet time (silence and solitude are appropriate synonyms) is an essential ingredient of a contemplative spirituality. We need some time without activity, without words, without people. We need these not to escape from activity or words or people, but to get our heads on straight and our hearts beating to the proper rhythm so that we can work creatively, so that we can speak wisely, so that we can deal with people gently and compassionately. Without some quiet time in our lives any kind of contemplative spirituality will quite simply be out of the question. It is *that* important. As Merton writes in *The Sign of Jonas:* "Those who cannot be alone cannot find their true being and they are always something less than themselves" (p. 262).

When Evelyn Waugh edited Merton's *The Seven Storey Mountain* for its British public, he changed the title to *Elected Silence.* It could be argued that this title, taken from a poem of Gerard Manley Hopkins, captured the meaning of the book better than Merton's title, which refers to the seven mountains of purgatory. In going to Gethsemani, he had elected an order, the Trappists, whose very name evoked a picture of quietness and silence: monks who never spoke to one another except in sign language. But Trappist life called for more than external silence. Merton had elected a life-style that required silence of the heart as well as silence of the voice.

Obviously you and I cannot elect silence in the same way and to the same degree as Merton did. If ours cannot be the high-octane silence of the monastery, it still remains that we need some quality silence or solitude or quiet time to fuel any kind of in-depth spirituality. Merton speaks of the creative power and fruitfulness of silence:

> Not only does silence give us a chance to understand ourselves better, to get a truer and more balanced perspective on our own lives in relation to the lives of others: silence makes us whole if we let it. Silence helps to draw together the scattered and dissipated energies of a fragmented existence. It helps us to concen-

trate on a purpose that really corresponds not only to the deeper
needs of our own being but also to God's intentions for us.
(*LL,* 43)

Solitariness

In talking about solitude, it is helpful to reflect on two
inevitable facts of human existence: (1) there are times when
we are alone; (2) there are times when we are in the midst of
people.

All human beings are solitary. Most people, though, are
averse to *being* alone or *feeling* alone (the latter is possible even
in a crowd). Yet however distasteful to us it many be, solitariness is an inescapable element of the human condition. No
matter how gregarious our lives may be, there will always be
those times—and they are by no means few—when we will be
alone. Perhaps it happens at night, when we cannot sleep. Even
if another may be sleeping at our side, we are still alone. Questions flood our minds: some petty and inconsequential, others
profound and inexplicable. We have to face them—alone. Even
in a crowd of people we can experience solitariness, as, for
instance, when we have no bonding with anyone who is there.
And if solitariness stalks us all through life, it makes its final
appearance at life's end. No matter how surrounded by loved
ones we may be, each of us dies her/his own death. We all die—
alone.

Human Society

The solitariness of our lives is complemented by that other
element that is part of human life: that we live in the midst of
people. We belong to human society. If that society develops
into *community* (where persons are respected for who they are
and where freedom and responsibility are highly prized) it can
give meaning to our solitariness: it can turn it into true solitude. In such solitude we experience the unitive relationship
we have with our sisters and brothers in that community.

On the other hand, society can degenerate into a mere *collectivity:* a conglomerate of individuals feeling their separateness, each motivated by self-serving concerns, each moving in disharmony toward separate, often conflicting, goals. Such a collectivity cannot know solitude. Consequently, it does all it can to avoid the solitariness that life imposes on us.

While the collectivity cannot offer us a way of escaping our solitariness entirely, it does everything it can to help us forget our loneliness. It seduces us into living fictitious lives: lives in which we are out of touch with reality and become victims of what Thomas Merton (in his "Notes for a Philosophy of Solitude," published in *Disputed Questions*) calls the "tyranny of diversion."

Diversion

The notion of "diversion" Merton has borrowed from Blaise Pascal. Pascal writes about *divertissement.* The word defies exact translation; but the term "diversion" is probably as accurate as any. Diversion means systematic and planned distraction, which makes it possible, as Merton puts it, for a person "to avoid his [her] own company for twenty-four hours a day" (*DQ,* 178). Diversion means engagement in inane activities that benumb our humanness. It is the constant turning to superficial or meaningless actions as a way to avoid facing the true realities of human life. We exhaust ourselves in our efforts to acquire things that advertisements tell us we must possess, knowing all the while that we are letting ourselves be duped by a commercialism that bombards us relentlessly and in all sorts of sophisticated ways.

Unless we are vigilant and on guard, we succumb to a life that is divided and fragmented, pulled this way and that by conflicting plans and projects. When this happens, we find ourselves so often doing things we don't really want to do, saying things we don't really mean, going places we don't really want to go. Merton is correct in describing diversion as "tyranny"; for it controls our lives and deprives us of the freedom to be our real selves.

The words Merton uses to describe what "diversion" leads to or what it springs from are illuminating: "illusion," "fiction," "stupor, "apathy." They evoke a vision of someone who is in a daydream, out of touch, in a daze. This is not to deny that such persons may seem to function very well on the surface, but they never reach the deeper realities of life, for these are precisely what diversion enables them to avoid. "The function of diversion," Merton writes, "is simply to anesthetize the individual as individual, and to plunge him [her] into the warm apathetic stupor of a collectivity which, like himself, wants to be amused" (*DQ*, 178). The soap operas and situation comedies of contemporary entertainment easily become an addiction. They readily take the place of the "bread and circuses" that served as the *divertissement* of ancient Rome. There was plenty wrong with Roman society and the Roman emperors offered the diversion of food and entertainment to make people forget the banality and meaninglessness of their lives. Our society does much the same and has ever so much more in the way of sophisticated technological tools for doing so.

The would-be contemplative renounces the call to live by diversion. He or she refuses to walk away from reality. Rather, they are determined to seek the truly real and to live with it, whatever may be the cost. They want to see life as it is, with all the absurdities that may entail. This means they face straight on the anguish of realizing that underneath the apparently logical pattern of a "well organized" and rational life, there lies an abyss of irrationality, confusion, pointlessness, and indeed of apparent chaos. The solitary person pricks the bubble of the tight, self-contained illusion that the devotees of diversion build about themselves and their little world. He or she is prepared to live with life's incomprehensibility rather than ignore it or pretend it isn't there.

This willingness to face reality bare-handed—with no gloves on, as it were—requires faith and at the same time makes true faith possible. For one of the essentials of interior solitude,

Merton writes, is that "it is the actualizing of a faith in which a man takes responsibility for his own inner life" (DQ, 180). Faith is a plunging into the mystery of life. When faith seeks to avoid that mystery by having recourse to conventional formulas without ever probing their meaning, *faith itself can become a form of diversion*. A faith of prepackaged, un-thought-out answers to all the important issues of life is a diversionary faith.

A person of true faith travels, not without difficulty, toward the heart of mystery. Such a person, as Merton puts it, works "his way through the darkness of his own mystery until he discovers that his own mystery and the mystery of God merge into one reality, which is the only reality" (*DQ*, 180). This reality is that God lives in us and we in God. Our heart beats in the heart of God. As Merton would say in Calcutta in October of 1968 (I have quoted this before, but it fits here too): "[It is] not that we discover a new unity. We discover an older unity. My dear brothers [and sisters] we are already one. But we imagine that we are not. . . . What we have to be is what we are" (*AJ*, 308).

The person striving to be a contemplative does not withdraw from the society of his sisters and brothers. What he or she does do is renounce the myth of unity that diversion appears to offer, in order to attain true unity in God. He or she looks toward a deeper and more real unity—a unity so profound that nothing divisive can ever reach it. "He [or she] seeks a spiritual and simple oneness in himself [herself] which, when it is found, paradoxically becomes the oneness of all men [and women]—a oneness beyond separation, conflict and schism" (*DQ*, 182). God is everywhere and all that is finds itself in God.

I have been relying a good bit on Merton's thoughts in his essay "Philosophy of Solitude." Let me try to sum up my thoughts on some of the things Merton is saying. He is telling us that there are three levels at which we can live. First, there is the phenomenal level, the level of what appears to be. It is the surface level, where harmony seems to exist or, if it doesn't, we are able to divert ourselves from the disharmony and live our lives insulated, as far as possible, from the disturbing, the troublesome, the burdensome. This is the *level of diversion*. At this

level people are not able, as T. S. Eliot says, "to live with much
reality." Or, as Merton puts it: "Most [people] cannot live fruit-
fully without a large proportion of fiction in their thinking"
(*DQ,* 187).

There is a second level of human existence, which might be
called the *existential level.* Below the surface realities of life, it is
the level where we are in direct contact with life's complexities,
disharmonies, incongruities, contradictions, and absurdities.
This is the level that the contemplative chooses to explore and
refuses to be diverted from.

The third level is the *contemplative level,* wherein a person
realizes his/her potential as a contemplative, breaks through
that level of seeming meaninglessness, and enters into the mystery of his/her own true self—and in doing so enters at the
same time into the mystery of God. It is here that the contradictions and absurdities of life find their resolution. This is
what Merton is talking about when he refers, in *Conjectures of a
Guilty Bystander,* to Julian of Norwich and her "eschatological
secret," namely, her deep conviction that "all will be well. All
manner of things will be well." The Lord comes to us with the
final answer to the world's anguish. The "Last Day" will bring
not destruction and revenge but mercy and life. "All partial
expectations will be exploded and *everything* will be made
right" (*CGB,* 212).

Merton sums up the contemplative level of life in this way
(and here he is obviously talking about the solitary in the
monastic community; but, *mutatis mutandis,* it can be applied
to any would-be contemplative):

> The solitary . . . lives not in a world of private fictions and self-
> constructed delusions, but in a world of emptiness, humility, and
> purity beyond the reach of slogans and beyond the gravitational
> pull of diversions that alienate him from God and from himself.
> He lives in unity. His solitude is neither an argument, an accusa-
> tion, a reproach or a sermon. It simply is. And therefore it not
> only does not attract attention, or desire it, but it remains, for the
> most part, completely invisible. (*DQ,* 184)

He also makes clear that going into silence is not escapism. Momentary retirement from life's normal round of activities has a very positive purpose.

> We do not go into the desert to escape people but to learn how to find them; we do not leave them in order to have nothing more to do with them, but to find out the way to do them the most good. [Yet even these purposes are secondary.] The one end that includes all the others is the love of God. (*DQ,* 80)

We live at a time when more and more people are becoming involved in all sorts of ministerial roles in the church. They especially need times of quiet and silence. As Merton writes: "Our service of God and of the Church does not consist only in talking and doing. It can also consist of periods of silence, listening, waiting. Perhaps it is very important, in our era of violence and unrest, to rediscover silent inner unitive prayer and creative Christian silence" (*LL,* 39). Those who exercise ministry in the church have need of silence, not in order to flee from the community they serve, much less to renounce it; rather, they see silence and solitude as a grace-filled opportunity to discover the deepest meaning of Christian community and their own identity within that community. Paradoxically, taking time to withdraw from community enables us to appreciate its importance. It puts us in touch with the God who gives us community and with our sisters and brothers who make up community.

> *How nice*
> *To be aware*
> *That God is*
> *Here and there*
> *And everywhere.*

Just Being: Luxury or Necessity?

The collectivity does more than entice us to follow the way of "diversion." It does its best to throw onto us a sense of guilt, if we dare to "take time out" from the relentless compulsion to "get things done." It tells us that quiet time, silence, solitude is wasted time, because it produces nothing. The collectivity will not allow us times just to "be." We must always be "doing" something.

Trying just to be has its cost. Any serious effort to make quiet time a constant in our lives calls for what may be a truly herculean effort. It's a wonderful, even attractive, experience, but how do I make it a reality in an already overly busy life? One speculative answer—which may not help much, but which sets a perspective—is to say: "We don't try to fit quiet time into our lives. We try to fit our lives into some quality quiet time." A fine-sounding principle, but the question that keeps shouting for an answer is quite simply How can I do this?

I recall a retreat that I gave recently to a group of graduate students from a Roman Catholic seminary (now a school to prepare lay ministers for the church). I made my pitch for the importance of making silence, solitude, quiet time a continuous, ongoing reality in our lives. One young woman expressed her complete agreement with all that I had said and then posed the problem she faces: "I have a husband, three young children, and a house to take care of. I have meals to prepare for my family and papers to write for my classes. Happily, I have a husband who carries his share of these responsibilities. But still day after day goes by when I can't get everything done that I ought to, to say nothing about finding time for quiet. I'd love to have solitude and silence in my life. But I don't seem able to manage it, at least with any sort of regularity."

I thought to myself: "Wow, if I could come up with an answer to her problem, I could write a best seller." (Just entertaining this thought momentarily undoubtedly shows how much I have let myself be caught up into a production-obsessive society.) But of course I had and have no answer for her, just a few suggestions that may or may not have been helpful. I offered them somewhat diffidently, because I was all too aware that I have nowhere near the kind of problems to deal with that she has. I am retired, a writer, a person who can largely arrange my own schedule. So I have no excuse for not having quiet time in my life. I offer my suggestions, therefore, with something of an apology for presuming to do so.

1. Have the conviction that some silence and solitude are important and worth struggling to achieve. There will be times when we have to lower our expectations. Instead of the half hour or twenty minutes a day (that would be our normal practice), there may be those occasions when the best we can do is to use the two or three minutes it takes to walk to our car or the brief time we spend waiting for someone to arrive or even the brief pause that might be involved in a change of activity. When this is the best we can do, let these be moments of quiet awareness.

2. Would it be possible to have some "family quiet time"? I ask this as one less wise, though it seems to me that, if this could be done [you tell me if it's possible or if I'm completely off my rocker in even making the suggestion], the ability to value silence would be one of the most precious gifts parents could bequeath to their children.

3. Be aware of what you are doing when you are doing it. So often when we do one thing we are thinking of what we have to do next or remembering what we did before. This scatters our energies. To be keenly aware of what we are doing (whether it's washing the dishes or cutting the grass or writing papers or carrying out the many other duties our life situation calls for) helps us to live less distracted lives and preserve a simplicity and a unity within ourselves that are a kind of lived inner silence.

4. We should not forget that fulfilling the responsibilities that each day brings us is doing the will of God. They are not to be seen as adversaries of silence and solitude. One way of helping ourselves realize this is to pause a moment, when changing from one task to another, just to be and to remember the presence of God. Such moments of awareness, brief though they may be, help nourish that inner unity within us.

5. Try especially to find some quiet time on Sunday. It is the Lord's Day. It is a day sacred to the mystery of the resurrection. In his unpublished work *The Inner Experience,* Merton writes of Sunday:

> We stop working and rushing about on Sunday not only in order to rest up and start over again on Monday, but in order to collect our wits and realize the *relative* meaninglessness of the secular business which fills the other six days of the week, and taste the satisfaction . . . of the peace that should filter through the whole week when our work is properly oriented.

6. Endeavor to arrange the activities you must engage in so that there can be some quality quiet time at least on one day of the month (or week?).

7. Get a copy of Jean François Millet's famous painting *Angelus* and place it in some conspicuous place where your eyes will be drawn to it regularly. The painting shows a man and a woman in the fields stopping their work for a brief moment to recite the Angelus prayer, which traditionally is said morning, noon, and evening. Presumably they had heard the Angelus bell ringing in a nearby church, calling them to a moment of prayer. I make this recommendation not as an incentive to move you to say the Angelus each day (though that would surely be a fine practice to adopt) but rather to suggest this painting as a visible reminder of the possibility, open to all of us, of saying short aspirations (one-liner prayers) during the day to remind us of the wondrous fact that we are always in the presence of God.

I bring this chapter to a close by offering a few sample aspirations, taken mostly from the psalms. If this practice proves helpful to you, you might want to make your own list of favorite one-liners, drawn from whatever sources you choose (the Bible, literature, books of spirituality). Be most free in choosing aspirations that best suit your spiritual journey toward wholeness.

A Brief Selection of One-liner Prayers

O God, be gracious to me and hear my prayer. (Ps. 4:1)

Lord, make clear your way before me. (Ps. 5:8)

Lord, heal me! (Ps. 6:2)

How great is your name, O Lord, our God, throughout the earth. (Ps. 8:1)

I will praise you, Lord, with all my heart. (Ps. 9:1)

My happiness lies in you alone. (Ps. 16:2)

Turn your ear to me, hear my words. (Ps. 17:1)

You make [me] glad with the joy of your presence. (Ps. 21:6)

The Lord is my shepherd. (Ps. 23:1)

Hear the voice of my pleading, as I call for help. (Ps. 28:2)

You are my hiding place, O Lord my God. (Ps. 32:7)

Like the deer that yearns for running streams,
so my soul is yearning for you, my God. (Ps. 42:1)

A pure heart create for me, O God. (Ps. 51:10)

O Lord, open my lips
and my mouth shall declare your praise. (Ps. 51:15)

In God I trust, I shall not be afraid. (Ps. 56:4)

To be near God is my happiness. (Ps. 73:28)

Lord, my God, let my cry come into your presence. (Ps. 88:2)

O give thanks to the Lord, for God is good,
for God's love endures forever. (Ps. 106:1)

My help shall come from the Lord,
who made heaven and earth. (Ps. 121:2)

Out of the depths I cry to you, O Lord,
Lord hear my voice. (Ps. 130:1)

I thank you, O Lord, with all my heart. (Ps. 138:1)

O Lord, you search me and you know me. (Ps. 139:1)

O Lord, lead me in the path of life eternal. (Ps. 139:24)

The upright shall live in your presence. (Ps. 140:13)

To you, O Lord my eyes are turned;
in you I take refuge. (Ps. 141:8)

Teach me to do your will, for you, O Lord, are my God. (Ps. 143:10)

You are close to all who call on you from their hearts. (Ps. 145:18)

I will praise the Lord all my days. (Ps. 146:2)

In your mercy keep us free from sin
and protect us from all anxiety. (Mass liturgy)

We wait in joyful hope
for the coming of our savior, Jesus Christ. (Mass liturgy)

Lord Jesus Christ, Son of God,
have mercy on me a sinner. (The Jesus Prayer)

(All psalm texts from Grail translation: London: Collins, 1963.)

CHAPTER SIX

Why Can't I Experience God?

ℊ

> Only the person who is free from attachment finds that
> creatures have become his friends. As long as he is attached
> to them, they speak to him only of his own desires. . . .
> When he is selfish they serve his selfishness. When he is
> pure, they speak to him of God.
>
> —Thomas Merton, *NMII*

Why is it that the world seems opaque to us? Why is it that it
is not translucent: if God is truly everywhere, why is it that we
are so forgetful of God's presence? What must we do to open
our inner eye so that the world may become what it really is:
that which reveals rather than conceals God? Or, to get back to
the Baltimore Catechism, can we find a better answer than the
Catechism gave to the question: "If God is everywhere, why do
we not see God?" What is it that gets in the way of our seeing
that God is everywhere?

One answer is that what gets in the way is quite simply—self.
If our spirituality is concentrated on self, even on self-improve-
ment, what we will continue to see is self, not God. This surely
is the reason for Jesus' insistent call to *denial of self.* Thus, Jesus
says in Luke's Gospel: "Those who wish to be my followers,
must deny *their very selves,* take up the cross each day and follow
in my steps" (Luke 9:23; see also Mark 8:34; Matthew 16:24).
The statement is in all the Synoptic Gospels. Denial of self, it
should be clear, is an absolute necessity for one who wishes to
follow Jesus and go with him into the vision of God.

Now I should warn you that, as you read this, your eyes could be playing tricks on you. By that I mean that you may think that what I wrote was *self-denial*. But that is not what I said. I said "denial of self." You may ask: But aren't they really the same thing: self-denial and denial of self? My answer is that they could, even should, be the same thing. But in Roman Catholic vocabulary and practice, at least, they really have been different for a very long time. By that I mean that we hardly ever talked about "denial of self"; almost always we talked about "self-denial." And "self-denial" conjured up special associations for many of us.

When we used the term "self-denial," it seemed to refer to things *outside ourselves:* giving up possessions or giving up certain enjoyments. Even if we spoke of giving up our desires, our own will, our own choices, we tended somehow to *objectify* these realities, as if they were somehow apart from us. We tended to see self-denial as denying ourselves *something,* rather than what Jesus is talking about: denying *our very selves.* To put it simply, our *self-denial* did not really reach our *deepest inner being;* yet that seems to be what Jesus is talking about.

Take, for instance, the way we used to practice self-denial during Lent. We certainly approached Lent with a spirit of fervor and generosity. We were eager to give up things for the glory of God and for our own growth in grace. I think we never quite understood what connection there was between our giving up a dessert and our getting grace. But it was something we really believed. Our Lents, however, often became endurance contests for us. We felt guilty if we had a dessert, and about midway during Lent we began counting the days until Holy Saturday noon, when, thank God, it would all be over for another year and we could once again indulge ourselves in the pleasures we had decided to give up for Lent.

My First Sin!

What I should do at this point is give you a very concrete illustration of what I mean. This is not easy for me to do. But I decided that the best illustration I can give of the point I am trying to make is to tell you the story of "My First Sin." (No, that's not the title of Fr. Greeley's latest novel!) Anyway, I blush to remember and even more to recount what I am about to tell you. It happened more than sixty years ago, but I still grieve about it and feel the need every once in a while to make public confession of it.

The time was Lent in the year 1924. I was a student in the first grade at St. Andrew's school in Rochester, New York. Our teacher, Sister Teresina, suggested to us that we ought to give up something during Lent. Her advice was that we give up candy. So I decided that was what I would do. And I did very well, until one fatal day when my mother and I were visiting some friends of the family. During the course of our visit I was offered a very special piece of candy that I was very fond of. It was called a maplene (mapleen?). I don't know how to spell the name or even if they are made any more. At any rate, I want to confess that I yielded to the temptation. I ate the maplene. You might say: "But that wasn't so bad." Ah, but that isn't the whole story.

When the last week of Lent came, Sister Teresina asked us how many had kept their promise "not to eat candy during Lent." I was faced with a terrible dilemma. I so much wanted to raise my hand. And at that moment, when I was seven years old, I was suddenly born as a moral theologian in the best tradition of casuistry. For in the split second between her question and the time I had to raise my hand, I reasoned that a maplene was really a very particular type of delicacy that no one in his or her right mind could possibly call by such a common and generic term as "candy." So I had not eaten *candy*. I had eaten a *maplene*. Hence I could raise my hand. I did. And I have repented many times since and asked for mercy.

I presume you are not too shaken by this revelation of my youthful duplicity. But it is a good example of the point I have been trying to make: that in (hopefully) bygone days, self-denial meant for most of us doing something that was *external* to ourselves that never really affected who we were. It did not touch our deepest inner self. *Yet this is precisely what Jesus is talking about in the Gospel.* He doesn't speak of denying ourselves something. He speaks of *denial of ourselves. Period.* He is talking not about something we have to *do,* but something we have to *be.* He is telling us that real denial of self can't be something simply on the surface; it has to reach into the very depths of our being. It involves a *metanoia,* a change that happens inside of us, that makes us think and act differently from the inside. *Denial of self* is not a matter of accumulating "brownie points" with God, to put it crudely. On the contrary, it is nothing less than a remaking of ourselves *from the inside* after the image of the Lord Jesus. It means getting rid of all that is false and phony, all that is unreal. It means giving up the desire to manipulate others and also giving up the willingness to be manipulated by others. It means recentering ourselves, making God and others, rather than our petty selves, the center of our lives. It means *building a spiritual spine* in order that spiritually and morally we are able to stand on our own feet, not needing to be propped up all the time by institutional structures.

Denial of self really means denying the false self in us, so that our true self may emerge. Our true self is in Christ. Our true self is in God. When we have sloughed off this false, superficial self—and indeed when we are in the process of sloughing it off—we discover that our true selves are one with God. The world then ceases to be opaque. It no longer hides God. God becomes transparent in our world and especially in our own selves. The denial of self leads to the affirmation of the self we truly are and always have been in God—only it has been hidden from us for so long.

When we speak about denial of our false self and affirming of our true self, we are at the very heart of the challenge of Christian faith. And never perhaps in the church has it been more important for us to find this inner reality, this personal center, this depth which is within us.

I firmly believe that in the present situation that exists in the Roman Catholic Church, the only ones who are going to survive are those who have discovered their own deep inner life and are able to stand on their own feet. We live in a time when tensions and disagreements are sharply dividing people in the church. Only the spiritually mature, who are in touch with their deepest inner self, will be able to remake the church, so that as God's pilgrim people it will be better able to do its part in transforming hearts and in shaping a new world order, in which justice, equality, peace, and nonviolent love will prevail—in a world where people truly care for one another.

The denial of self that Jesus calls us to has precious little to do with giving up desserts or candy (even maplenes). It has everything to do with the transformation of hearts and the unveiling of our own inner self.

Discovering My True Name

If denial of self seems to carry negative connotations, another—perhaps more positive—way of expressing the same truth is to say that the great Christian task we face is the task of discovering *our own true name*. In a certain sense that is what salvation means: coming to know my true identity, coming to know my name. What I want to suggest to you is that there is a difference between *my names and my name,* that is, between the names that *correctly describe* me and the name that *truly defines or identifies* who I am. All my life I need to look hard and honestly at my names—that is, my correct names, those that correctly define me. I must do this so that I can eliminate those names that conflict with my true name and enhance those that accord with my true name.

What is the difference I am drawing between my *correct names* and my *true name?* My correct names are those qualities and characteristics—good and bad—which describe me in the human community. There are many correct names that can be applied to me: names that describe aspects of my personality that I project on the world around me. Some may be good aspects of my person: that I am loving, thoughtful, generous, outgoing. Other of these names may designate negative and even harmful aspects of my person—that I am violent at times, that I am selfish, that I like to manipulate people to my own purposes. Both the positive and negative descriptions may be correct, though fragmentary, statements about me. Thus, my "correct" names are always in the plural. They are many. They partially reveal and partially conceal my true name.

My true name is something quite different. It is not multiple; it is singular. There is only one. For my true name expresses who I am, not in fragmentation but in unity. My true name expresses my Truth and that Truth is one. *My true name is known in its fullness only to God.* My great task in life is to discover my "true name" and come to know how it differs from my "correct names." In the book of Revelation, the Risen Jesus speaks to the church at Pergamum and says: "To the victor I will give a white stone upon which is inscribed a new name, known only by the one who receives it" (2:17). Ultimately I can find my True Name only in God. For God alone holds within the very Divine Self the secret of my true identity. As Merton puts it: "I break through the superficial exterior appearances that form my routine vision of the world and of my own self [the sphere of my "correct names"], and I find myself in the presence of hidden majesty" (*NSC,* 41).

The experience of Christian conversion and growth is our daily effort to *move from our names to our Name,* from the fragmented qualities that describe what I seem to be in the world to the unity that names the reality that I truly am. Identifying our correct names, that is, discovering what is true and what is false in me is a step toward the self-knowledge that eventually will enable me to discover my true name: the name God gives me, the name that expresses the truth God wishes me to embody. I move from the fragmented qualities that describe what I seem to be in the world to a unity of my personhood that names the reality that is my unique truth and identity.

Some of you, I am sure, are acquainted with the writings of the Vietnamese Buddhist monk Thich Nhat Hanh. I once heard him give a talk entitled "Non-Violence in a Violent World." He centered his talk on a poem he had written. The poem was entitled "Call Me by My Correct Names." The poem tells of a twelve-year-old Thai girl who had escaped from Thailand in a small boat. There was also on the boat a sea pirate. The pirate raped the young girl, and in her despair she threw herself into the sea.

In his poem Nhat Hanh identifies himself with the girl who was raped. We can do this too, because we are often victimized and manipulated by people. But the poet goes further: he also identifies himself with the pirate who raped the girl. "I am also," the poet writes, "the sea-pirate, my heart not yet capable of seeing and loving." But there is more: he speaks of other names that could correctly describe him. "I am the child in Uganda, all skin and bones," but also, "I am the merchant of arms selling deadly weapons to Uganda." And he piles names one upon another: the repressive government official, the man dying in a forced labor camp.

The poem is most moving. For it helps us to realize that each of us is both oppressed and oppressor, the victim and the persecutor. We are wounded by others; yet we also wound others by what we say and do. Sometimes we suffer violence; sometimes we inflict it.

This is why I suggest that our spiritual task is to identify our correct names; to find out which of them is true and which is false. Identifying our correct names is a big step toward self-knowledge that eventually will enable us to discover our true name: the name known to God, the name God gives us, the name that expresses uniquely who we are in wholeness and unity.

When I discover my true name in God, I discover relationships. I discover my oneness with all my sisters and brothers. It is possible for me to be unjust or violent or unkind to others when I relate to them only at the level of my "correct" names. At the level of the true name—both mine and that of my sisters and brothers—I must love them with an unconditional love. For they are my other selves. When I relate to others at the level of my true name, I am able to release into the world the dynamism, the dynamite, the divine power of Love.

When God created me, God gave me my *true name*. All my life God has been calling me by my true name. So often I have not heard it, because I have not really been listening. Sadly, many people never hear their true name till death. For when God calls us to the ultimate vision of God's presence, God calls us by our true name and we hear at last. That is one way of understanding death: it is, finally, hearing our true name spoken.

What we need to do is to hear our true name now. This requires —we have already discussed this earlier—that we live more on the inside than on the outside. Remember the old song "Laughing on the Outside, Crying on the Inside"? Often we can be so occupied with what is going on on the outside, that we miss the experience of our inner depth, where alone we can find God and our true self, our true name. A poet described the plight of modern mortals when he wrote: "Always looking out; never looking in." This looking in is what can happen in quiet prayer, in moments of silence, when we *let go of all our correct names* and *allow ourselves simply to be in the presence of God*. Contemplation is being called by our true name and hearing it at last. Being boxed in by surface, external realities often puts us, without our realizing it, between narrow walls. To find the depths of our being is to overcome that narrowness. A Welsh poet, Waldo Williams, has written: "What is life? It is finding a large room between narrow walls." That large room is where we find God and all of reality and come to know the essential oneness of all. Merton writes: "If I penetrate to the depths of my own existence and my own present reality, the indefinable 'am' that is myself in its deepest roots, then through this deep center I pass into the infinite 'I Am' which is the very Name of the Almighty." And in discovering that Name, I discover my own true name.

> *What's in a name?*
> *A rose is a rose*
> *Is a rose.*
> *But a name may be*
> *Correct but not true.*

For a correct name
Is true
Only on the surface,
Not in the depths.
The true name is
Always deep, deep, deep.

If everyone in our world would listen, if we all came to hear our true name, we would replace the violence that is so prevalent in our world with the peace of unconditional love. We would replace oppression and manipulation with deep respect and concern for the dignity and worth of every person. We would see the divine image in one another. Our world, which so often is opaque, would become translucent with the presence of God. God is everywhere in our world. It is charged with God's presence. Let us look at our correct names, which describe us only on the surface—those names that can create narrow walls. But most of all let us seek for the large room where we hear our true name, which unites us with the Divine: not only with God but with the divine in everyone we meet. If we could really see one another as we really are, we would want to fall down and adore, so dazzled would we be by the wondrous image of God in everyone.

Jesus and the Need to "Let Go"

Finding our true name requires a great deal of something I have already mentioned, namely, "letting go." The words "letting go" have a special resonance for me. They call to mind a statement that I always find so moving when I read the passion narrative of the Fourth Gospel. Recall how people come to seize Jesus in the garden. Twice Jesus asks them: "Whom do you seek?" Each time they speak out the name they knew him by: "Jesus of Nazareth." And each time he accepts this name, which correctly describes him. He replies: "I am he." The first time they are awe-struck and fall to the ground. The second time he adds to the statement "I am he" words of protective concern for his followers: "If I am the one you seek, then *let these people go.*"

"Let these go." Think of what Jesus is saying and what it cost him, in this situation, to "let go." These are the men who were his closest companions for some three years. They were the ones whom at supper, just a few hours earlier, he had called not servants but friends. At the supper, we may wonder: Did he think of the first time he had met them? Did he go back to the moment when he definitively called them to be his disciples? He had spent the night in prayer. Then he called the ones he desired as his companions. Mark expresses it in this way: "He appointed twelve *to be with him* and to be sent out to preach and to have authority to cast out demons . . ." (Mark 4:13, REB).

He called them "to be with him." Despite his deep communion with his Father, Jesus was truly human. He needed people to be with him. He delighted in the companionship of those he had chosen. Sure, there were times when their dullness of perception amused him, times when their pettiness exasperated him. But he loved them. He was happy that they were with him. There were deep bonds between Jesus and his chosen ones.

Now he is in danger—danger for his life. He is being taken into custody. He will be surrounded by people who hate him, despise him, want to be rid of him. If ever he needed his friends "to be with him," it was now. Yet what does he say? "If I am the one you seek, then *let these go.*" He does not look at his friends and say: "Stay with me." No, he looks to his captors and tells them: "Let these people go." And once they had leave, they all fled. And he was alone—among people who wanted to destroy him.

Yes, it surely was difficult for him "to let go" and be alone. Yet we need to remember that "letting go" was not a new experience for him. He had already done it many times—and done it so well. Remember his ministry in Galilee: how, at first, everyone was acclaiming him."They were astonished at his teaching. For he taught as one who had authority, and not as their scribes." And recall how one evening in Capernaum, after he had cured Peter's mother-in-law, when the sun was setting, the whole city gathered outside the door and he healed their sick. And they hailed him as a wonder-worker. On another occasion he had to get into a boat to preach, so great was the pressure of the crowds that came to hear him. The people were filled with awe and admiration. Never before had they seen such extraordinary things. Surely God was in this man, they thought. Was he maybe the one who would deliver Israel from the Romans? On one occasion he had to flee into the mountains, because in their enthusiasm they wanted to make him king.

Yet not all were impressed by him. Some saw him as a threat to the established order. They could not countenance his casual attitude toward their traditions. They could not understand this man who failed to keep their fasts, who violated their sabbath laws, who said things about God and told parables about God's love and mercy that did not square with the old-time religion.

Nor were these opponents without power. They succeeded in turning the popular mind against him. He had *to "let go" of success and popular acclaim*. He had to "let go" of good name and reputation.

Surely this was not easy. It must have been a joy to him to see that his mission had been going well, that people were listening to him, that they heard what he had to say about God's loving compassion. Jesus was human. It is human to want to be liked by people. And Jesus had to "let go" of this very human need.

The Epistle to the Hebrews says that he prayed "with loud cries and tears to his Father, who could save him from death." Indeed, God could have answered Jesus' prayer and saved him from death. But God did not. Jesus had "to let go" of what he expected from his Father. How difficult for anyone who is human to "let go" of what one expects from God—especially when what one expects seems to be so good and right. Yet Jesus "let go" of his expectations.

Indeed, it was God's will that he die. He "let go" of life. He consented to his death. After a lifetime of "letting go," he had given all. There was nothing left for him "to let go of."

One way of reflecting on Jesus' life is to see it as a process of "letting go." He "let go" until there was literally nothing left. He was living out his own words that the only way you can save your life is to lose it: save it by giving it away. He gave so completely of himself that there was nothing of himself left. There was only God. That is why some scholars want to say that it was in his death-resurrection experience that Jesus came to know himself as God. This is a difficult topic to talk about. For we are in an area of reflection where words falter and are forever inadequate. Nor do we need to strive to make them adequate.

Perhaps it is enough to say that Jesus had his act together. He was fully and totally himself. He went to his death the freest person in all the world. Nothing finite, nothing created, nothing human enslaved him. For he had "let go" of everything. That is why I say "there was only God."

We need to see that it is "hanging on" that is slavery; hanging on to anything that is sinful, petty, selfish, violent, even anything created, human, finite. It is "letting go" that makes us free.

"What is it that enslaves me?" I have to ask. Maybe it's a desire to have my own way all the time. Maybe it's a hidden anger or bitterness that I nurse and won't even talk about. Maybe it's that violence I have discovered in my own heart and am ashamed of, but do nothing to get rid of. Maybe it's that I'm too comfortable and satisfied—content with my lot and not really concerned that more than half the world goes to bed hungry and that millions of people in the Third World are continually being oppressed by a government I elected but am not really trying my best to influence, or by multinational corporations that I buy goods from because I get a bargain.

My spirituality ought to concentrate more on God than on myself. Yet I do need to take a look, at least briefly, at the things that enslave me, the things I need to "let go of." For they are the things that make the world opaque, so that I cannot know my true name and therefore cannot see God. Letting go of all the things that enslave me is one way of discovering an answer to the question: If God is everywhere, how can I experience God?

CHAPTER SEVEN

Violence and the Different Ways of Dealing with It

Power always protects the good of some at the expense of all the others. Only love can attain and preserve the good of all.
—Thomas Merton, *PFP*

American violence is the necessary and inevitable expression of our conflict between our declared principles and our utter failure to live by them.
—Thomas Merton, *Syracuse Notebook*

The scene is a small town in the western United States. The town has but one main street. It is midday. People line the street on either side, but the street itself is empty—except for two men who face each other. Each has his hands on his hips, but in such a way that you cannot see whether they have guns or not. The men are perhaps two hundred yards away from each other. Slowly they begin walking toward each other. All at once each of them removes his hands from his hips. They approach closer and closer to one another. . . . Then they reach out their arms and embrace one another. They are friends.

Now I want to ask you: Did you expect the story to end that way or, more likely, were you expecting a shoot-out? Are we so conditioned by the many western movies we have seen—with shoot-outs of this sort—that we have almost lost the ability to imagine this kind of scene as peaceful rather than violent?

Emotions Engendered by Violence

It seems as if somewhere in our psyche there is a strange fascination with violence. It horrifies, yet at the same time it allures. It is worth pointing out that what I have just said about violence is exactly what Rudolf Otto has said about God: God is *mysterium tremendum et fascinosum,* a mystery that causes us to tremble, that frightens us, yet at the same time draws us, attracts us. In people enthralled by a prize fight or a wrestling match, in those who crowd around an accident or those who during the Persian Gulf War found themselves glued to their TV sets, in people devouring every detail of the horrible story of a mother who drowned her two little children because her new boyfriend didn't want to deal with a family—in these and many other cases we see the fascination that violence engenders. We are drawn to it almost irresistibly at the same time that we are repelled by it.

Mixed in with feelings of being allured by violence and being repulsed by it is also the experience of compassion and concern for the victims of violence. Anyone who does not have a hardened heart is moved and touched by the suffering that is caused by violence. Much of the world grieved when so many people (many of them students) were killed in the Pan-American plane that was bombed to pieces in midair over Scotland in December 1988; and there was a deep swell of compassion in 1990 for the heroic young people in China who so courageously faced violence and death in the hopes of bringing freedom to their country. People open their hearts to the victims of hurricanes and floods, and they open their checkbooks too. A whole nation grieved at the terrible destruction of life that took place in Oklahoma City in April 1995.

To fascination and compassion must be added confusion and bewilderment: not knowing how to deal with terrorism in the Middle East, genocide in Yugoslavia and Rwanda, so much bloody slaughter in Haiti and in so many other places in the world.

The Mystery of Violence

We need to speak about the mystery of violence. It's as old as Cain and as new as Saddam Hussein. The mythical tale of Cain in the book of Genesis is a frightfully moving and upsetting story. Its intent is to show how humankind first experienced death. It is a story that points to the fragility of human life. *Hebel,* the word for Abel in Hebrew is the word that Qoheleth uses in the book of Ecclesiastes for all that is vain. *Hebel* means "vanity," "vapor," "that which is and quickly disappears." The death of Abel is the symbol of the frailty of the lives of men and women. Even Cain will become *Hebel,* the "vapor," that will disappear. But in the Genesis story he is first a murderer.

We have all heard many times his response to God's question: "Where is your brother Abel?" Cain replies: "I do not know. Am I my brother's keeper?"

My Brother's (or Sister's) Keeper?

This statement of Cain has often been used to show that we are indeed responsible for our brothers and sisters, and this surely is true. But there is a deeper meaning to the text. The word "keeper" in the Bible is *shomer.* In one form or another it is used some 450 times in the Old Testament. Yet there is not a single instance in which it is used to describe a social obligation that one human person has to another. When humans are described as "keepers," it is usually a matter of property or livestock over which they have custody, for example, a keeper of the flock. In the rare instances where it means one man "keeping" another, it may refer to a servant who acts as a bodyguard or it may mean "detaining" a person, that is, keeping a person in custody. But never is it used to refer to the care and concern we owe our brother or sister.

It is only God, as lord and ruler over the whole universe who is called the "keeper" of human beings. "The Lord is your keeper. The Lord is your shade at your right hand." "Behold he who keeps Israel will never slumber nor sleep." "May the Lord bless you and keep you. May he let the light of his face shine upon you."

The point I am making is that the narrator of Genesis assumes that the reader understands that Cain is not God and, therefore, not the keeper of his brother. He is not being charged as one who has the responsibility of being his brother's keeper. But the story is more subtle than this. Cain's answer to God's question "Where is your brother Abel?" is a downright lie. He knows perfectly well where his brother is. He left him lying dead in a field and has no reason to believe that he has moved in the meantime. When someone tells a lie, seldom is the liar content just to tell the lie. Usually there is some effort to defend one's falsehood. So, in the awkward silence that follows his denial that he knows anything about his brother's whereabouts, Cain feels obliged to say something more. So he adds the question: "Am I my brother's keeper?"

It is an infuriatingly clever question. It is saying in effect: Can I be expected to play the role of God? Can I be expected at any moment to know exactly where my brother is? To do so I would have to follow him every moment. Then I would *have to be* looked upon as "my brother's keeper." Note how he pretends a certain moral sensitivity. "I would not want to usurp the place of God." Yet it's a pretense and a ploy. Abel could not have suffered any more from having Cain as his keeper than he did from having him as his brother.

And there is a sense in which his denial that he is his brother's keeper also embodies a lie. For by taking the life of his brother, he was claiming to have the right over the life of another. And that is a right that belongs only to God. God gives life. God sustains life. And when the time comes, God calls people to death and new life. Only God has the power of life and Cain usurped it. Despite his denial, Cain chose to play the role of "keeper," a role that belongs only to God.

Violence as the Desire to Control

We need to realize that this story is mythical: that is, it is a story set in primeval times intended to shed light on present human existence. What it tells us is that, while we have the obligation of care and concern and love for one another, we must never attempt to assume total authority over others. We should never try to be another's "keeper." When we agree to help people in need, it must be a response to their need without any intent on our part of taking control of their lives. This is true whether it is the poor we are helping to get food, jobs, and so on, or minorities whom we are aiding in their attempt to achieve equal rights and opportunities. We have to avoid the desire to control, to want to solve their needs in our way—which really means doing violence to them. Unless we avoid all forms of paternalism or any attitudes of patronizing, we are, whether we realize it or not, seeking to act as their "keeper." We think of them as in a zoo and ourselves as their "keeper." May I say that *there is a bit of Cain in all of us.* It's so easy to want to run people's lives. Murder is the ultimate expression of that desire to run people's lives or have them pay the consequences. And on a more extensive scale, war is an expression of the same desire. It is a nation playing the role of Cain and, like him, usurping the right of God. All too often our country, protecting multinational interests, has played the role of Cain to the nations of the Third World.

Violence as Injustice

This desire to control others, to bend them to our will, is seldom exercised in a gentle way. Almost always it becomes violence, which is essentially destructive power directed against the human person. Whether it involves specific *acts of injustice* or *situations of injustice* produced by such acts, its intent is to *deprive* human beings of their freedom and their rights and, if deemed necessary, of their lives. Violence can destroy groups of people. As I mentioned above, all America was aghast at the wanton destructiveness and loss of life brought about by the bombing of the Federal Building in Oklahoma City in April 1995. And the Holocaust is a grim example of violence against an ethnic group. Violence can destroy or enslave whole nations, and the ultimate violence is the nuclear holocaust that could destroy the world as we know it.

Violence exists where there is a difference between a *good that could be* and *an evil that actually exists,* and it is *violence* that stands in the way of that possible good being realized. Violence enables the actual evil to perdure. For example, when families live in abject, dehumanizing poverty, decent living for them *is* a possibility. The forces that prevent them from achieving that possibility and realizing a decent level of living are the forces of violence.

Violence may be personal (one individual victimizing another), or it may be structural, built into the structures of a system (whether that system be the laws of the land, the operations of multinational corporations, the freedom-denying character of certain institutional structures). Violence may be physical (doing harm to a person's physical well-being) or it may be psychological (brainwashing, breaking a person's spirit and his/her psychic well-being).

Violence When I Am Not Aware of Being Violent

There are other forms of violence that can be a part of daily life without our really being aware that violence is taking place. The violence of *the evil* may do the greatest harm; but it is the violence of the good that can be a daily drain on us. There is the violence *on the highway.* Why is it that the most gentle persons become demons when they get behind a wheel? There is violence on the telephone or in conversations. In some cases I may be acting or thinking violently and no one else knows; but I know. There is the violence of forcing people to accept your way of doing things.

Violence in Speech and in Accepted Practices

There is the violence done to something very preciously human, the power of speech: the violence of misusing words, using words to deceive, turning words into a lie. Political campaigns often use language that shows contempt for the truth. So does much commercial advertising. The recent movie *Quiz Show* tells the sad story of Charles Van Doren, a young professor at Columbia University. He was the winner on a quiz show, answering the most difficult questions with ease. The truth finally came out that he had been given the answers beforehand. The revelation of this deception tarnished the Van Doren name made so famous at Columbia by Charles's father, Mark Van Doren. Thomas Merton wrote to Mark, who had been his teacher at Columbia and offered his sympathy. He pointed out that Charles was as much victim of society as its deceiver. He pointed out how deception is a normal part of much commercial advertising. Well-known people appear on commercials and receive huge sums of money for endorsing products they may never have used. This is deception, but one all too readily accepted. Few people would think of accusing such "advertisers" as frauds and liars, even though their language does violence to human speech.

There can be violence in any number of accepted practices. The attitude toward women in the church is often a form of violence, as also the attitude of many Roman congregations of the Roman Curia toward theologians. There can be violence in preaching. I have a feeling that many sermons on sexual morality are often the articulation of violence.

Violence of "Accumulation"

One of the subtle forms of violence that is endemic to our Western culture is the tyranny of accumulation. We live in a culture which, for reasons of increased productivity and greater profits, keeps inventing needs for us and convincing us that we owe it to ourselves to fulfill those needs. The tyranny of accumulation does violence to our own integrity (by moving us to succumb to a false value system) and perhaps to the well-being of others (whose life situation at a poverty level I might help to improve, if I used my relatively comfortable resources to help meet their basic needs rather than my own more superficial ones).

We begin to realize the violence to people that excessive accumulation causes, when we discover that in the United States, as of the last figures available, the wealthiest 1 percent of American households owns nearly 40 percent of the nation's wealth; and the top 20 percent have more than 80 percent of the country's assets. During the year 1989 (the most recent for which figures were available), 100 percent of the increased wealth in the United States went to the top 20 per cent of American families. These figures are scary. The tyranny of accumulation does grave violence to the poor.

Violence in Activities

In his book *Conjectures of a Guilty Bystander,* Merton points to a form of violence that we don't often advert to: the violence we do to ourselves for overwork, by overactivity. He writes:

> Douglas Steere remarks perceptively that there is a pervasive form of contemporary violence to which the idealist fighting for peace by non-violent methods most easily succumbs: activism and overwork. The rush and pressure of modern life are a form, perhaps the most common form, of its innate violence. To allow oneself to be carried away by a multitude of conflicting concerns, to surrender to too may demands, to commit oneself to too many projects, to want to help everyone in everything is to succumb to violence. More than that it is cooperation in violence. The frenzy of the activist neutralizes his own inner capacity for peace. It destroys the fruitfulness of his own work, because it kills the roots of inner wisdom which makes work fruitful. (p. 86)

Keep in mind that I am suggesting that violence is always in one way or another a desire to control that overflows into abuse of persons (and that person may even be oneself!)—a failure to respect persons, their rights, their minds, their hearts, their bodies, their total being.

Sometimes
I'm violent
and know it.
Sometimes
I am violent
And I don't know it.
But it's still
Violence.

Three Ways of Dealing with Violence

There are different ways of dealing with violence and the suffering it causes: (1) passivity, (2) counterviolence, and (3) nonviolence.

Passivity

We can close our eyes to what is happening and try not to get involved. This is often confused with a peaceable attitude, when in fact it is an attitude that gives support to violence. It is passivity that makes it possible for dictatorships to flourish. People take refuge in passivity for a number of reasons. They may not be directly affected by the violence and prefer to take the easy way out—realizing that if they enter into the struggle, their lives will be changed, perhaps even endangered. Or people may choose the path of passivity because of *fear.* They know that if they speak the truth they will have to suffer the consequences. They may be made to suffer even more than what the violence presently inflicts on them. They may lose their jobs. Their families may be threatened. In addition, passivity may be the reflection of an attitude of helplessness. "I am only one person: what can I do?" Or "we are not people of influence. What can we do against a well-built system of injustice? Besides, we lack the know-how to act creatively." It is to foster this sense of helplessness that repressive governments do their best to keep people illiterate and therefore unequipped to organize themselves effectively to oppose violence.

If we remain passive in the face of violence and let violence grow, our very passivity is a form of collusion with those who do violence and want it to continue. *Passivity* is the lowest form of reaction to violence. Gandhi saw it as assuming the posture of a slave. The book of revelation has some dire words for those who, when faced with a situation of evil, are neither hot nor cold. Yet passivity can be a perennial temptation. It is so easy just not to act, to keep out of things. We have to fight passivity all our lives.

Counterviolence

A second way in which we can respond to violence is by counterviolence. People who become aware of injustice and the need to do something about it often resort to counterviolence, because they know of no other responsible way to react. This is *a big step up* from the way of passivity. It expresses a desire to *take responsibility* for an intolerable situation. The pages of history down through the ages are bloodied by the struggles of counterviolence reacting to violence. While the choice they have made is not one that I would want to choose, I know that I must respect such people and the honesty with which they have entered into the struggle for justice.

Yet, without in any way feeling that I have the right to judge, much less to condemn, those who see counterviolence as the means to overcome violence, I still want to ask questions about the means and look at what I believe are the evils it brings in its wake.

I recognize that it is instinctive to want to preserve ourselves, our group, our nation. This instinct, which we share with the animals, is a normal life-preserving reaction. We don't want to suppress it, but rather channel it into *creative* ways of self-preservation. Children use counterviolence when faced with aggression. Thus, if Billy takes Johnny's toy away from him, Johnny may well get a couple of friends to give him additional strength so that he can get his toy back. But what we need to see is that this additional strength, which forces Billy to return the toy, involves an *escalation of violence*. And you can conceive of Billy then going out and getting five of his friends to help him get the toy again. What this simple example illustrates is that *counterviolence always escalates the spiral of violence*. Inevitably, then, the logic of counterviolence is that you must always be physically stronger than your aggressor—which means you have to enter into the spiraling of violence. So, in the nuclear race (which has not really subsided for a true "peace dividend") each side pretends that it is weak, so as to build up the forces of violence.

Another problem that counterviolence raises is this: if I am willing to use the same "weapons" as the aggressor, I am letting the aggressor dictate the means I shall make use of. I allow myself, in other words, to be infected with the disvalues that necessarily accompany violence. This, I believe, is one of the fundamental arguments against the death penalty: it justifies the very conduct it seeks to condemn, namely, violence. Embracing counterviolence forces me to give up some of my own values. Inevitably there will be a lessening of regard for the human person. And the more the violence escalates, the more moral compromises I have to make. Let's not forget that as a country we entered World War I "to make the world free" and ended up with the fire-bombing of noncombatants in German cities, and World War II was brought to a terrifying conclusion with nuclear bombing of innocent civilians in Hiroshima and Nagasaki. *Letting violence escalate corrodes the moral character of a person or of a nation.*

More than that, counterviolence diminishes the sense of true community. It ignores the fact that true change cannot be imposed. So if you try to introduce a new system into a society by counterviolence, you have already planted violence into the new system you are trying to create. All too often those who win find they will need their own secret police to impose change on those who were not willing to change. True change can occur only if hearts and societal structures are changed. Counterviolence suffers from the same inhumanity that marks all violence. It never reaches the root out of which violence grows.

Nonviolence

A third approach to aggression and violence is active nonviolence. This was the way of Gandhi, of Martin Luther King, Jr., of Thomas Merton. But, what is more important, it was, I believe, the way of Jesus of Nazareth. This brings us to a central theme of this book: one that will be discussed in subsequent chapters.

CHAPTER EIGHT

Nonviolence: A New Level of Human Consciousness

Conflict will never be abolished but a new way of solving it can become habitual.

—Thomas Merton, *PFP*

The perspectives of the non-violent have to be enlarged in all directions, so that it becomes a genuine and profound spiritual movement and a force for life in a really rotting and corrupt world.

—Thomas Merton, *HGL*

Mount Carmel is a huge promontory jutting into the Mediterranean Sea near Haifa in Israel. It has sheer drops to the sea on the west and into the Valley of Jezreel on the east. The word "El" in Carmel is the Hebrew word for God. Carm-el, therefore, means the vineyard of God. Mount Carmel is a place of lush, luxuriant growth. In the Bible it is a symbol of beauty. In the Song of Songs, the lover says to his bride: "Your head rises like Mount Carmel." Not exactly the kind of compliment a lover would pay to his beloved today. But he is not saying: "You have a big head"; rather, he is saying: "You are a picture of sheer beauty like Mount Carmel."

I recall being on Mount Carmel several years ago. There is a church honoring the Virgin Mary on the top of Carmel. I climbed to the roof of the church. From that position I could see the whole Valley of Jezreel spread out before me. Shaped like a triangle and about fifteen miles wide, it is of great impor-

tance historically. Through this valley passed the armies of
Assyria, Egypt, and Babylon. So did the armies of Alexander
the Great and, much later in history, the armies of Napoleon.

It was a very clear day; and looking to the east I could see the
mountain on which the village of Nazareth is built. It was a
great thrill to realize that Jesus, when he was a teenager, could
look out from his backyard and see this valley that had been
and would continue to be one of the great battlegrounds of history. History had been made in this valley, because some of the
great and decisive battles of history had been fought there.

Isn't it strange that we tend to read history as principally the
narrative of wars? If we were asked to tell our own history as a
nation, we would probably say we came into existence through
a war, the Revolutionary War. We remained a single nation
because of a very bloody war, the Civil War. In this century we
fought a world war "to keep the world safe for democracy,"
only to fight a second one less than a generation later. This Second World War ended with the guilt of the nuclear destruction
of Hiroshima etched indelibly on our national conscience.
Then there was an utterly fruitless and savage war fought in
Vietnam. And, just recently, the Persian Gulf War, in which,
besides the deaths of our own service personnel, thousands
and thousands of Iraqi women, children, and elderly people
became what our armed forces, with its disinfected and euphe-
mistic language, referred to as "collateral damages."

The Great Lie of History:
Conflict Is Inevitable

Why do we tell our history in terms of wars instead of in
terms of times of peace? The reason is, I believe, that we have
come to accept that the story of human civilization is the story
of a series of wars, separated by brief periods of uneasy peace.

We have accepted the notion that war, whether hot or cold, is
the normal human situation. In a word, we have accepted the

inevitability of war and the impossibility of any real permanent peace.

When preparations were being made for the Persian Gulf War, there were many people opposed to it; but their voices were drowned out. They might have thought with the psalmist: "Too long have I had my dwelling among those who hate peace. I am for peace; but when I speak they are for war" (Ps. 120:6–7, NRSV).

Not long after the American "victory" in Iraq, I saw General Colin Powell on television. He was asked what was happening at the Pentagon, especially in this time when the Cold War seemed to have come to an end. His answer was: "We are preparing for the next war. We don't know when it will be or where it will be. But what we do know is that there will be war." The irreversible inevitability of war has been the great curse of human history. The feeling that there must be war—sooner or later.

The Greek and Latin Words for "Peace"

This sense of war's inevitability has made its way into the words we use for "peace." Our Western world is, in the main, a product of the Greco-Roman civilization. It is instructive to note how the Greeks and the Romans spoke about peace. The Greek word for peace is *eirēnē*. It is a word whose meaning tends to be negative. *Eirēnē* describes an interlude of nonstruggle in the midst of what is the normal human condition: war. *Eirēnē*, therefore, has more the sense of a truce between wars, not an end to war. *Eirēnē* is a "peace" that accepts the curse of the inevitability of war.

The Latin word for peace, *pax,* has a slightly more positive meaning: it suggests a "pact," "an agreement" not to fight for the time being. It is a state more or less fragile that exists for a time in the midst of ongoing struggle and strife. It too accepts the belief that war is inevitable.

The Hebrew Word for "Peace":
What a Difference!

There is, however, a word—a word that comes not out of our
Greco-Roman culture but out of the culture of the Hebrew
Scriptures, a Hebrew word—that refuses to accept the inevitability of war. That word is *shalom*. *Shalom* is able to reject the
inevitability of war, because it gives a strongly positive content
to peace. *Shalom* means "wholeness," "completeness." People—
whether as nations or as individuals—are at peace when they
achieve wholeness, when they realize their potential for goodness and love and truth and justice, when they become who
they really are and who God intended them to be. When we
become fully human, we must reject war and enmity and ani-
mosity, for all these things are dehumanizing. They make us
less than human beings. War dehumanizes us. Enmity and ani-
mosity toward others dehumanizes us; and when they de-
humanize us, they deprive us of peace.

Shalom is an important word in the Bible. Yet the people of
Israel realized that they had not achieved wholeness. They
were not fully what they ought to be. They believed that they
once were whole. They believed also that they would *once again*
be whole—but that time was *not yet*. In other words, they saw
the full reality of *shalom* as God's gift in the beginning: paradise was the place of peace. They also saw it as God's eschatological gift at the end. Thus, *shalom* was an elusive reality for
them. That is why Isaiah could speak of beating swords into
plowshares and Joel of beating plowshares into swords. *Shalom*
was in the beginning. It will be at the end. But it is not now. That
seems to be the message in the Hebrew Scriptures.

Jesus and Shalom

It is in the New Testament that *shalom* becomes a reality that
is not only primordial and eschatological but existential. *The*
heart of the New Testament message is that the radical possibility of

peace has entered our world in Jesus Christ. In a remarkable passage in Ephesians (2:11–22), Paul says Jesus Christ *is* our peace. He has broken down the dividing wall, the hostilities that have separated us; for he has made both of us into one.

When Paul spoke of Christ making the two of us one, he spoke of the only world he knew: one divided into Jews and Gentiles. He could not have known the full import of his words. Jesus came to break down the barriers that separate all peoples, not just Jews and Gentiles. He is the one who comes to reconcile the First World and the Second World and the Third World. Paul could never have expressed it in that way; even you and I could not have expressed it that way even a few decades ago.

The Dawning of a New Human Consciousness

The human race has grown mightily in its insights in a relatively brief period of time. In our own century we have reached a point in the evolutionary process where we have come to see human beings and human relationships in an entirely different way. We realize that, for our very survival, we have to take a global view of the human race. We have come to see that our fate is bound up with the fate of peoples throughout the world. The human race has shrunk to family size. Whether we like it or not, we are all part of one family traveling through space on our tiny planet Earth.

Never before in human history has there been such a perception of *human solidarity and oneness.* Our experience as a human community has taught us that our only salvation is to respond to Jesus' call to communion—a world communion. To choose the alternative—to choose separateness—is to choose disaster and destruction. As a world community, we must work for that complete well-being, for all that is embraced in *shalom:* a well-being that is bodily, spiritual, societal. We must become whole. We must become complete. We must become what God wills us to be.

I believe that as a human race we have entered into a whole

new state of consciousness. A new understanding of who we are and who we are called to be. This new heightened state of consciousness of human solidarity is God's gift drawing us into God's *shalom* in a way that may not have been possible for past generations.

> *Reader, do I know you?*
> *Do you know me?*
> *I am you.*
> *You are me*
> *(though strict grammarians would*
> *Want me to say: You are I.)*
> *Yet one though we are,*
> *We are distinct.*
> *Mystery? Yes, as*
> *God is Mystery.*
> *For we*
> *(Grammarians too)*
> *Are all*
> *One in God.*

We have to see our part in this dramatic plan of God to make us all one. We have to begin by building true communion wherever we are. If we have in our lifetimes seen war so many times in the world, we have equally seen enmity and strife and hatred and hurtfulness in our own midst. We have to rid ourselves of the terrible curse of inevitability: the defeatist attitude that would say that we cannot change from our pettiness, our bickering, our finding fault with others, our hurting them, our harsh words, our tendency to judge others and find them wanting. Another way to put this is to say that not-loving is not inevitable.

For Jesus has brought into our world the reality of unconditional love. And unconditional love is at the root of *shalom: God's unconditional love for all God's people and our unconditional love for one another.* Because of that love we dare to hope for true shalom in our time.

The Role of the Poor
in This New Consciousness

I mentioned earlier the human tendency to write our history as if it were simply the story of battles and wars. In addition, it must also be said that we tell our history as the story of the great and the mighty: those who appear to have changed the face of history. As Hildegard Goss-Mayr has said: "the history we learn at school is the history of our violence and our 'heroes' are the most violent of them all" (*Non-Violent Life Style,* 79).

But there is another side of history: a side that gets scarce notice at all; and that is the saga of the poor, the marginalized, the oppressed, the victims. Their story is the dark side of history that never seems to emerge in the telling of it.

In 1968 in the city of Medellin, Columbia, a gigantic step was taken to rectify this one-sided view of history. The bishops of Latin America, in asserting that both church and world must give a "preferential option for the poor," opened up a whole new aspect of that "heightened human consciousness" to which I have referred. It is not just that we can no longer ignore the poor and the oppressed in telling the human story. On the contrary, we must view what happens to them as being at the heart of the story of our humanization: that process whereby we achieve that truly contemplative vision that we are all one in God and that each human person has a unique and inviolable dignity. A true reading of history cannot ignore the daringly bold words of the Mother of Jesus, who could also look out upon the Valley of Jezreel from her Nazareth home:

> God has brought down the powerful from their thrones,
> and lifted up the lowly;

> He has filled the hungry with good things,
> and sent the rich away empty. (Luke 1:52–53, NRSV)

Joan Chittister, O.S.B., tells how these "little ones of God" are leading the way toward this new consciousness:

The little people who faced the dogs in Selma to gain their humanity, the tiny women who climb the fences of nuclear installations to pray for their dismantling, the little groups who sign petition after petition to stop planetary pollution, the little boats that obstruct the wanton killing of dolphins and whales, the myriad little people who refuse to be willing victims of an age more given to death than to life—these are seeds of a new human consciousness, a new global soul." (From preface to Gerard A. Vanderhaar, *Active Non-Violence: A Way of Personal Peace*, vi)

Yes, as Jesus looked over the Valley of Jezreel from his village of Nazareth and realized the destruction of human life that had occurred there with such regularity, he knew that he must preach the kingdom of God as a kingdom of peace. He knew that he must call to people to be peacemakers and assure them that they would in a special way be called the children of God. And it was his vision that the bloody battlefield of Jezreel need not be that would move him to say to us today: "Rid yourselves of your terrible weapons of war. A half century ago, you exploded the first nuclear bomb. Since then, your weapons have become so fearfully destructive that they are able to destroy you and your world." "Do not let yourselves be held captive," Jesus would tell us, "by the *Great Lie of history:* namely, the terrible Lie that tells you that wars are inevitable, that they must be."

More and more people today are hearing words of this sort coming from the gospel. More and more people realize that our future and that of our children and our planet depends on our abolishing war. More and more people are ready to heed the words of John Paul II: "War is totally unacceptable as a means of settling differences between nations. War must be consigned to the tragic past of history. It should find no place on humanity's agenda for the future."

> *Jezreel is a*
> *Place of*
> *Many wars.*
> *How odd.*
> *For Jezra-El*

Means "God sows."
God sows
Only peace.
"Now is the seedtime of peace."

What I am suggesting is that we are finally finding in the gospel something that was always there, but which for various reasons remained hidden from us till now. What I am referring to is the *nonviolence that Jesus taught and lived.* What is far more, we are discovering that the nonviolence of Jesus must be seen, not just as an approach to war, but—even more—as a way of life that must affect everything we do.

It took many of us a long time to come to this nonviolent commitment as a life-style. After all, we have been brought up for some fifteen hundred years or more with the theory of the just war. While we have been trained not to be violent in our actions, we have also been clearly taught that force may be met with counterforce, if the force being used against us is unjust. Nonviolence, we were told, was an ideal way of acting in certain circumstances; but there were many situations in life in which it would prove impractical and undesirable. It was at best a compartment of the Christian life. We are just now beginning to see nonviolence as a life-style that touches every aspect of what we do and think and judge.

A nonviolent life-style demands great discipline. A person who wants to walk the way of nonviolence must purify himself or herself of the hidden aggressions that are so often a part of us without our even realizing it. We have to empty ourselves of ill will and hostility toward an oppressor. Nonviolence may call for us to suffer for the well-being of others.

What is most important is that we see nonviolence as a way of life that, if it is to be real, must enter into all our relationships. People will sometimes ridicule nonviolence by asking: How can one try to act in a nonviolent way toward a Hitler or a Saddam Hussein? That is always a good trick to use for avoiding moral obligations: turn the obligation into a speculative case. In our daily lives, it's not Hitlers and Saddam Husseins we are confronting. It's the people we live with and work with.

Most of them would surely not qualify as enemies, but there may be times when they seem to approximate that. This is the challenge the gospel of *shalom* presents to us: to make nonviolent, unconditional love a way of life that is truly inclusive. Learning to be nonviolent in lesser matters can prepare us eventually to be nonviolent in greater matters.

Let me express this very positively: we have come to realize that nonviolence does not exist simply to declare war wrong. It exists to declare that unconditional love, which is at the root of *shalom,* is always and everywhere right. A nonviolent stance in life calls me to commit myself ever more fully to that kind of love.

Unconditional love is love that makes demands on oneself more than on the other. It is a love that brooks no "if" clauses. It does not say: "I love you, if you do this or that." Instead it says: "I love you regardless of what you do or say. I love you because, no matter what you say or do, you are the icon, the image, of God. Precisely because I love you, I will confront you with the truth and challenge you with its demands. But I will also be a listener. I will try to hear what you are saying. For I realize that I do not possess all the truth; and there may well be things you have to say to me that I need to hear. But regardless of how much we may differ, I shall try always to remember the contemplative vision: that you and I are one in God. That oneness exists at a level of perception that perhaps we do not often enough achieve. But I know in faith that that oneness is a reality. And since we are one, I must love you as my other self. There can be no strings attached to my love for you."

Nonviolence is a light that illumines life. It helps me to understand in a totally new way what it means to be a person. It opens to me a new way of dealing with persons, especially in conflict situations. It is the way of being a person and dealing with persons that Jesus taught by word and example. It is the only way we can make sense out of his challenge to love "our enemies" and to "do good to those who hate us." This is a contemplative intuition. For we are one even with "enemies," since we are all one in God.

The youthful Jesus looking over the Valley of Jezreel from
the mountain of Nazareth saw in his imagination a bloody field
of war and slaughter. On the mount of the Beatitudes he had
another vision—one he bequeathed to us: the vision of a world
at peace, the vision of a world where there would be no more
war, no more hatred, no more cruelty, a world in which the
resources of the world would not be squandered and polluted
and people would not be manipulated—for the sake of material
profit. A world wherein people would care for one another and
listen to one another. It's the kind of world of which Isaiah
speaks, where "justice will bring about peace and right will produce calm and security" (32:17) and where "my people will
abide in a peaceful habitation" (32:18).

Thomas Merton presents a striking description of this new
vision in one of his *Freedom Songs.*

EARTHQUAKE

(. . . Isaiah 52)

Go tell the earth to shake
And tell the thunder
To wake the sky
And tear the clouds apart
Tell my people to come out
And wonder

Where the old world is gone
For a new world is born
And all my people shall be one.

So tell the world to shake
With marching feet
Of messengers of peace
Proclaim my law of lov
To every nation
Every race . . .

For the old world is ended
The old sky is torn

Apart. A new day is born
They hate no more
They do not go to war
My people shall be one.

So tell the earth to shake
with marching feet
of messengers of peace
Proclaim my law of lov
To every nation
Every race.

There shall be no more hate
And no more oppression
The old wrongs are done
My people shall be one.
                              —*CP*, 701

CHAPTER NINE

Nonviolence and the New Testament

¶

Jesus lived and died in vain if he did not teach us to regulate
the whole of life by the eternal Law of Love.
—Ignatius Jesudasan, *A Gandhian Theology of Liberation*

Some time ago *Commonweal* carried a heartwarming story of
a little girl's tiny steps in liturgical growth. At breakfast one
morning her mother gave her the usual bowl of cereal. She
held out her hand to her mother and said: "Beast." The mother
welcomes this expression of cordiality but was puzzled. "What
did you say?" she asked. The child extended her hand again
and said: "Beast." More bewildered than ever the mother
asked: "What do you mean, dear?" "Oh, you know, mommy. It's
what we say in church when we shake hands."

The little girl didn't quite catch the meaning of the gesture
of peace that takes place at a Catholic Mass. As children often
do, she tried her best to imitate what she saw adults doing. The
one thing she seemed sure of was that it was a rather nice thing
to do in the context of a meal. One can wonder whether there
may not be quite a number of adults who are not much farther
along than this little girl in their appreciation of what this gesture is intended to say. It is not meant to be the equivalent of a
back-slapping greeting at a Rotary club meeting. It has a rich
meaning that goes right back to that foundational truth we discussed in the introduction: namely, the resurrection of Jesus
from the dead.

The Easter Greeting
of the Risen Jesus

The peace greeting of the Mass actually picks up the first words of the Risen Jesus, as he "dropped in" on bewildered and terrified disciples in the upper room (where they had shared a meal before his death): "Peace be with you." I must confess that when I read this passage in John's Gospel, I can't help picturing Jesus with a big grin on his face, as he surprises them with the totally unexpected. In saying this, though, I must make immediately clear that I do not in any way want to make light of this event; I'm simply saying that, being truly human as he was, Jesus must have been tickled to break in on his slow-to-learn disciples in this unlooked-for way. But I do indeed want to emphasize that this event is one of immense import: this greeting at a joyful reunion that brought healing and restored wholeness to afflicted and broken disciples. The simple greeting, "Peace be with you," was loaded with meaning. He was saying to them: "You are forgiven and reconciled. You are saved and made whole. I embrace you with the unconditional love that you witnessed in my life and in my death, and that I shall continue to extend to people in the new immortal life I now live. I give you in its fullness all the wondrous promises that *shalom* implies." As his meaning gradually sank in, were some of the disciples, I wonder, moved to exclaim: "Wow!"?

Someday, I hope, the little girl will understand the deep experience of *shalom* that should be ours when we celebrate the peace (not "beast") ceremony in the Mass. Perhaps adults too, who know the right word, will experience (as I suspect many do not today) the deepest meaning of *shalom* when they exchange that sign of peace that traces its origin to the Easter event.

Jesus' Gift of Shalom

It may well be that the best way of making that *shalom* gesture at Mass mean more to us is to reflect on the light of *shalom* that shone across the life of Jesus as we meet him in the New Testament. Luke draws open the curtains on his narrative of the Jesus story with angelic choruses chanting: "Peace (*shalom*) to those on whom God's favor rests" (2:14). During Jesus' public ministry, there were the many times—some recorded, some not—when Jesus spoke to people with all sorts of afflictions these simple, powerful words: "Go in peace" (e.g., Mark 5:34; Luke 7:50). Read Jesus' farewell discourse in John's Gospel. The atmosphere of the upper room is peace, and peace is the message. "Peace I leave with you; my peace I give you" (14:27). "I have said this to you, so that in me you may have peace" (16:33).

The only way to that true peace that is *shalom* is the way of unconditional love. And, as I have already suggested, the other side of the golden coin of unconditional love is nonviolence. For those who wish to follow Jesus, nonviolence has to be a life-style that guides all our actions.

Sermon on the Mount
Sermon on the Plain

A brief look at that great charter of Christian disciples—what we call the Sermon on the Mount in Matthew and its parallel, the Sermon on the Plain in Luke—will make clear Jesus' plea for a life of nonviolence leading to *shalom*.

The Sermon on the Mount in Matthew begins with the beatitudes. "Beatitude" means happiness and the beatitudes point the ways—strange to our ears, surely—that will lead to that fullness of life and joy we call happiness. One of those ways is "peacemaking." "Blessed are the peacemakers, for they will be called the children of God" (Matthew 5:9).

The Sermon on the Plain, while it does not have the beatitude of the peacemakers, follows its own list of beatitudes (and woes) with a plea for people to listen. And what are they to listen to? These strong, challenging words (which the majority of Christians through the centuries have managed to ignore): "Love your enemies, do good to those who hate you, bless

120 NONVIOLENCE AND THE NEW TESTAMENT

those who curse you, pray for those who mistreat you" (Luke 6:27–28; see also a similar command in Matthew 5:44).

Actually, there are three forms of the "love command" in the Gospels. First, there are the words of Jesus about the greatest commandment, which he identifies as "Love God above all and love your neighbor as yourself." This is a general statement of the Christian responsibility to love. Second, there is the very specific command that relates the disciples of Jesus to one another. Jesus says: "My command to you is that you love one another, as I have loved you." Finally, there is this difficult command to love those whom, it would seem, we ought surely to be exempted from any obligation to love. Yet the command is there: "Love your enemies."

The first two love commands make a great deal of sense. Even for pragmatic reasons, it makes sense to love those with whom we live in proximity. It makes for harmony and concord in society. The command that disciples should love one another as sisters and brothers and do so following the example of the unselfish love of Jesus, while it may be difficult and demanding at times, also makes sense. For disciples of Jesus are called to imitate him.

But the command "Love your enemies" does not, at least on first hearing, make any sense at all. It seems to go against fundamental principles of justice. It seems to go against the obligation we have to love ourselves and not allow ourselves to be victimized by others.

And the maddening thing about it is that it is so all-inclusive. When you look at this command, whether in Luke or in Matthew, the command is always stated in the plural: "Love your enemies." The command of neighbor love, on the other hand, is always in the singular. From a purely human point of view, it would be much simpler if we could reverse these two and thus be allowed to choose which enemies we would find it expedient to love and love our neighbors in an abstract plural. If we could do that, we would be able to divide enemies into "personal," "political," "national" and any additional categories we might want to set up. Yes, it would be a lot easier to deal with this command, if we could pick which enemies we would love and which we would feel free to clobber, if we thought it necessary to do so.

And I might say that, when we haven't ignored this command entirely (which is too often the case), we have, in practice at least, diluted it. For we have decided that we do have to be sensible about this and realize that there must be certain types of enemies that we can exclude. We are inclined to think: "Jesus certainly could not have meant Hitler or Saddam Hussein, or even Rush Limbaugh or Newt Gingrich (if you happen to be a Democrat). We can't be expected to love people such as these." And the reply we get from the gospel is like the refrain used by one of our local banks in its television ad telling about services so unique and special that its customers are moved to say: "Surely I can't get *that* kind of service just from a bank"; and the ad says right back to them: "Oh, yes, you can."

Sorry, but there is no way of getting around these words about love of enemies, no way of diluting them: they call us to treat all persons, even enemies, with nonviolent love. They call us to a vision that is contemplative: a vision of the oneness we share with all God's people, even those who fit under the rubric of "enemy."

If the Easter greeting was a "wow" statement, "love your enemies" is an "ouch" statement ("ouch," according the dictionary, being a word that expresses sudden pain or displeasure). There is little comfort in these words of Jesus, only challenge. For they call us to love those we might quite understandably consider outside the pale of our love.

And let us be clear about what is meant by "enemy." We miss Jesus' point until we put a face and a name on "enemy." It is easy to love our enemy as long as the enemy is faceless or cloaked in an anonymous abstract plural. It is only when "enemy" takes on the visage of a particular person, someone I know, someone who has hurt me or mistreated me—only then that I begin to feel the challenge of Jesus' call to love that person, to pray for him or her. As I write this, I can think of just such a person whom I need to love and pray for. Is this perhaps your feeling as you read this and come face to face with Jesus' words and realize that they may perhaps apply to a particularly difficult instance of relationship you may have to deal with?

On 11 April 1968, June Yungblut, a close friend of Coretta King, who had been with Coretta since the terrible day of the assassination of Martin Luther King, Jr., wrote to Thomas Merton describing the funeral. She told him how, after the funeral, Ralph Abernathy's children asked Andrew Young "if they could hate the man who killed Uncle Martin?" Before Young had a chance to reply, Dr. King's two children (Martin and Dexter) spoke up: "No!" they said, "You can't hate him." And they gave their reason: their daddy had told them that they were not to hate anyone. They had learned well the lesson their father had taught by word and example: love is all-inclusive.

> *Who's that enemy*
> *I saw you praying for*
> *last night?*
> *Why would you do*
> *Such a thing?*
> *You're a Christian,*
> *You say?*
> *What's that got to do*
> *With it, anyhow?*
> *I'm a Christian too,*
> *But you don't see me*
> *Doing weird things*
> *Like that.*

Ways of Dealing with People

Actually, when he talks about relationships, Jesus speaks of three different ways of dealing with people: (1) retaliation, (2) reciprocity, and (3) God's way.

Retaliation

The way of retaliation is what is known as the *lex talionis*, the law of *talis*, which literally means the law of "such as" or "just like." What it means is that the gravity of the punishment should not exceed the gravity of the evil done. It means getting even, evening the score: taking an "eye for an eye and a tooth for a tooth."

It is worth noting that this law of retaliation was a very primitive way of trying to establish some kind of equity and righteousness in human relationships—this before there were any such things as courts of law, to which a person could appeal if she or he were wronged. What it meant, in practical terms, was this: if you did something nasty to me, then I or my family or my clan would be justified, indeed in some way obligated, to make a similar return to you. The purpose of this primitive way of administering justice was to curb excessive revenge. Its intent was not simply to say that your retribution for a wrong done to you must be "such as" the wrong itself; more importantly, its intent was to say that your retribution could *not exceed* the wrong that was done to you. Retribution must be "such as," not "more than."

In the Sermon on the Mount, Jesus explicitly rejects retaliation as a way of dealing with people. He says:

> You have heard that it was said, "an eye for an eye and a tooth for a tooth." But I say to you, "Do not resist an evildoer. But if anyone strikes you on the right cheek, turn the other also; and if anyone wants to sue you and take your coat, give your cloak as well."
> (Matthew 5:38–40, NRSV)

Jesus' directive to us is that we must not retaliate. We must forgo revenge. He orders us not to resist an evildoer. It is important to note that *he in no way commands us not to resist evil. This we must always do.* But our resistance is directed not against a person (whom we must always respect, no matter what she or he has done); rather, our resistance is directed against what that person has done. We must not let our conduct be determined by the conduct of those who treat us badly. A follower of Jesus must not be moved to hostility by a wrong done to him or her. This should not be taken, however, to imply passivity in the face of evil. The concrete picture of turning the other cheek is not meant as a directive to invite people to continue doing evil to us. Rather, it is an exaggerated way of saying: no revenge, no matter what. In fact, when Jesus was struck on the cheek in the court of the high priest, he did not literally turn the other cheek. Rather, he did what that symbolized: he confronted the high priest's servant with the truth: "If I have done evil, tell me what it is. If I have not, then why do you strike me?" He called his assailant to reflect on what he had actually done.

Reciprocity

A second way of handling human relationships is the *principle of reciprocity*. This means that I choose to treat people the way I would like to be treated by them. This principle—more humane than the principle of retaliation—also has a long history. It was expressed some five hundred years before Christ by Confucius. He put it in a negative way: "Do not do to others what you would not want them to do to you." This negative way of stating the principle implies the more positive expression that we find in Jesus' words in the Sermon on the Plain (in Luke): "Do to others what you would have them do to you."

Because we tend so often to be selfish, the principle of reciprocity can at times be very demanding. Precisely because we have the strong tendency to make ourselves the center of our universe, it not infrequently happens that we would like to be treated better than we treat others. And we would hope that others would have the good sense to see that they ought to treat us better than we treat them!

We should not, then, belittle reciprocity as a way of dealing with human relationships. It would make life much easier if reciprocity prevailed in friendships, in family or community relationships, in business relationships, and so on. After all, the principle of reciprocity can be seen as an application to our relationships of the command to love your neighbor as yourself. If we love our neighbors as ourselves, we would want to treat the neighbor as we would like to have ourselves treated. And Jesus accepts this principle. He says, in Luke's Gospel, "Do to others as you would have them do to you."

Yet while approving of reciprocity, Jesus went on to a yet

higher mode of treating other people. He made the point that even reciprocity can become self-centered. "If," he said, "you do good to those who do good to you, what credit is that to you? For even sinners do the same" (Luke 6:33).

God's Way

Jesus goes on to offer us a third way in which we can regulate our social relationships. He challenges us to treat people as God treats them. This is the highest and most demanding way of acting toward others. And it is the way to which Jesus and the gospel call us.

How does God deal with us? I think it can be said that the essential relationship of God as Creator to God's creatures is nonviolence. Created things (trees, animals, planets, persons) exist because God lets them be. God cooperates with them, keeping them in existence, sustaining them but never doing violence to anything God has made. *And the nonviolence of God flows from contemplation,* namely, God's total awareness of all that is and of the inseparable oneness of all that is.

The Nonviolent God

God is nonviolent and contemplative, because God is fully and totally and always who God is. This is what Matthew means when he calls God perfect. The Greek word that is translated as "perfect" means "wholeness." It means always being totally oneself. God is always true to the divine Self. God is never false to God's own reality and the reality of all created things in God. God, it could be said, "embodies" *shalom.* For *shalom* means a state or condition of wholeness and completeness. Ultimately, the call to nonviolence is indeed a call to peace; for it is a call to wholeness—a wholeness that means being one with God, in harmony within oneself, in communion with all of God's creatures. Nonviolence, in other words, means recovering the contemplative consciousness that we are all one in God.

It is worth our while to compare Matthew's statement about

perfection with Luke's parallel. Where Matthew says: "Be perfect as your heavenly Father is perfect," Luke puts Jesus' challenge in different words: "Be compassionate as your Father is
compassionate." This seems to make the ideal a little more
attainable, but it means the same thing. Compassion is a true
awareness (and therefore a contemplative experience) of our
sisters and brothers), in which we are in communion with them
through a spirit of nonviolent, unconditional love.

One other aspect of God's nonviolence toward us that is frequently mentioned by Jesus is *God's willingness to listen* to us. All
through the preaching of Jesus runs the refrain: "Ask God for
anything in my name and God will give it to you." Jesus keeps
insisting: Ask and you shall receive. Ask continually and often.
What he is saying is this: God is a good listener.

To sum up, nonviolence means unconditional love. And
unconditional love includes compassion and the willingness to listen
to others. Compassion is the ability to enter into the suffering
of another and experience it from the inside. We can have compassion even for those who do evil; for they suffer from a blindness and a darkness that prevent them from seeing the truth.

Dialogue and Nonviolence

We also have to be *willing to listen*. We have to acquire the
ability to enter into dialogue with people with whom we disagree. Dialogue has as its goal a sharing of the truth. It is not
just that I want to share my truth with another. It is also that I
want to share the truth the other has that I do not have. It is so
easy to be convinced that I am right that my mind may be
closed to what the other has to say. When this happens I don't
really hear what the other is saying. I simply wait until they have
had their say and then proceed to "set them right." There are
two people I know who especially love to talk. When they get
together, they vie with one another for the floor. You may
know people like that. What they are engaged in is almost

simultaneous monologue. They suffer through what the other says, so that they may have their own say. But they don't really *listen.*

Listening, truly listening, really hearing what the other has to say, is at the heart of true dialogue. It can oftentimes be a very enlightening experience. It can open up perspectives that had never occurred to me, because I had never before heard the other's position presented in his or her terms. Often when I truly listen to what they have to say, their position turns out to be quite different from the version of it I had in my own mind. Listening may show that we are closer to one another than we thought. Dialogue can be an opening up of what had seemed to be closed frontiers. It can be an enriching and rewarding experience.

The Woman Taken in Adultery

Jesus not only taught us to be nonviolent in our relationships. He showed us, in his own encounters with people, what it meant to be nonviolent. Consider the story of the woman taken in adultery narrated in chapter 8 of John's Gospel. Interestingly, this story made its way into the Gospel only with some difficulty. Some manuscripts do not have it. Does this suggest perhaps that the early church, like Christians of later times, found the nonviolence of Jesus more demanding of disciples than they were willing to accept? As the story is told, a woman is brought to Jesus and made to stand before everyone, as Hester Prynne in Hawthorne's novel is made to stand on a platform to display to all the scarlet letter on her breast. They ask him about capital punishment for this woman. (Where one wonders was the man? Adultery does require two.) The Mosaic Law prescribed stoning to death for one found guilty of adultery. What does Jesus think, they want to know. Jesus stoops down and writes on the ground. Why does he do this? Is he perhaps getting out of the way so that the woman's accusers are forced to look at the woman whom they have made to stand before Jesus? Does he want to make them see her simply as another human being and not as a legal case to be resolved by applying the law? At first Jesus is silent.

They keep pushing him for an answer. Finally he speaks and makes them confront their own violence. He will not allow them to hide in the anonymity of a crowd. If a crowd throws stones, then it is the crowd that is responsible, but no individual is identified as the killer. He forces them, individually, to see what their violence is leading them to do: "Let anyone among you who is without sin be the first to throw a stone at her."

When they heard these words, "they went away, one by one, beginning with the elders." Then Jesus, who had been writing on the ground stood up and faced the woman: "Woman, where are they? Has no one condemned you?" She answered: "No one, sir." And Jesus said: "Neither do I condemn you. Go your way, and from now on do not sin again." There is here no softness on sin. There is loving compassion and concern for the sinner.

The Parable of the Rich Man and Lazarus

The above narrative about the adulterous woman tells how Jesus protected this defenseless woman from the violence of those who were eager to punish her. It is a story that deals with violence in action. But there is another kind of violence that, at first hearing, one might not think of describing as violence. It is the violence of being blind to the needs of the poor, the oppressed, the disadvantaged. Jesus told a parable about this kind of blindness: the parable about the rich man and Lazarus, the poor beggar (Luke 16:19–31).

The rich man dressed in fine clothes and ate sumptuous meals every day. Lazarus, a poor, sick beggar in tattered clothes and with a body covered with sores used to come each day to watch the rich man at his posh table. He tried to catch the crumbs that fell from that table. The rich man did nothing at all to alleviate the sorry state of Lazarus. He didn't even see him there. Eventually the rich man died and went to hell, where he suffered great torments. Lazarus died and was carried away by the angels to be with Abraham.

Martin Luther King, Jr., in the last sermon he gave before his assassination, commented on this parable. He spoke of the "long-distance" call between heaven and hell, as the rich man pleads with Abraham. Dr. King pointed out that we must not see this conversation as a rich man talking to a poor man. On the contrary, Abraham was the richest man of his day. The conversation, he said, was between a millionaire in hell and a multimillionaire in heaven. The point he wanted to make is that the rich man did not go to hell because he was rich. He went to hell because he did not realize that his wealth was his opportunity. It was his opportunity to bridge the gulf that separated him from his brother Lazarus. His problem was that he did not see Lazarus as a brother. In fact, he did not see him at all. He allowed his brother to become invisible. One of the worst expressions of violence against the poor is to forget they are there, to ignore that they are brothers and sisters whom we must love with a love that displays itself in deeds on their behalf.

The Parable of the Loving Father and His Wayward Son

Jesus left no doubt that the unconditional love he practiced was a revelation of the God he came to tell us about. Nowhere is this clearer than in the three parables that make up chapter 15 of Luke's Gospel: the lost sheep, the lost coin, and the lost son. The last we call the parable of the prodigal son; it is better understood as the parable of the loving father.

To understand Jesus' intent, we need to keep in mind the context in which Luke places these parables. Think, for example of the parable of the prodigal. It is so exquisitely beautiful a story that we are often tempted to deal with it all by itself.

Then we have a wondrous story, but may miss the point Jesus is intending to make.

The story is Jesus' response to the stern criticism leveled at him by the Pharisees for associating with sinners. Their attitude was that good, religious, God-fearing people simply would not keep the kind of company Jesus did. Jesus' answer is clear and simple. I am with these people because I want to be like the One I call Abba, Father. The God I have come to tell people about is not an angry God. He is not a God of wrath. He is a God who is an Ocean of Mercy. And that does not mean that on occasions God shows mercy. Rather, Mercy is what God is. Compassion is what God is. When we see Mercy and Compassion, Jesus is telling us, we know that we are in the presence of God.

The God Jesus reveals is above all a God who reconciles, who wants always to unite us to God's very Self and unite us with one another also. Even when our God judges, it is as a reconciler. For when our God judges us it is not to punish us but to judge that we need God's Mercy. God wants to flood our lives with this divine Mercy. If judgment sometimes seems to be punishment, it is never God who punishes. It is rather that we can punish ourselves by closing the door of our hearts to God's Mercy. But that Mercy is always there—awaiting our acceptance.

Is this not the unforgettable picture we see in the parable? The father of this wayward lad is presented as single-minded: only concerned to have his son back. We can picture him standing on a hill outside his home, his hand shading his eyes from the setting sun, as each day he waits and peers hopefully down the road.

Then one day he sees what he has been longing for: his younger son coming back to life. Rushing to meet him, he doesn't even let the young man get through the confession he had been so carefully and anxiously rehearsing all the way home. The father scorns his request to be treated as a slave. A ring is put on his finger and shoes on his feet (slaves did not wear shoes). It is a never-to-be-forgotten scene: sheer mercy, transparent love, and unconditional forgiveness shine ecstatically through the story.

This is the way you are to think of God, Jesus tells the religious leaders of his day; and he says the same to us. There is no machismo, no arrogance, no spitefulness in the God I preach, only the purest unconditional Love. That is why I call God Abba.

What he taught about God was so new and so revolutionary that the religious leaders of his day could not accept it. In telling this parable Jesus signed his death warrant. His understanding of God was on a collision course with the understanding of God current among the religious leaders of his day. One of them had to die. Jesus went to a violent death because the God he taught about is a God who is supremely nonviolent. But God vindicated Jesus. By raising him from the dead God placed a seal of approval on what Jesus taught about God.

Jesus would not allow anyone or anything make him forget the inviolable dignity of every human person. He refused to fight violence with violence. His only weapons were truth and love. He told Peter—the impetuous disciple who wanted to fight it out in the garden—to put away his sword. Otherwise, like all who use the sword, he would perish by the sword. Surely his finest hour came when, hanging in agony on a cross to which he had been unjustly nailed, he cried out to his Father for those who had so wrongly oppressed him: "Father, forgive them, for they do not know what they are doing." His willingness to suffer for love is a vivid portrayal of what is surely the noblest moment of nonviolent love in the pages of human history. And it led to risen life.

When I read the Gospels today, it seems to me that it is difficult to do so with an open mind and fail to come face to face with the imperative of nonviolence. I most firmly believe that this emphasis has always been in the Gospel, though I must admit that it has only been in the last few years that I have discovered it there and come to realize its meaningfulness in my life.

If you and I embrace nonviolence as a way of life, we would be able to release into the world a power that nothing can ultimately withstand. It is the greatest healing, purifying, unifying power in all the world. For it is a divine power, the power of absolute love. Nonviolent love, on our part, is a way of letting God into God's world. It is opening the world to God's Spirit and God's love.

CHAPTER TEN

A History of Christian Attitudes toward War

> There can be no question that unless war is abolished, the
> world will remain constantly in a state of madness and des-
> peration in which, because of the immense destructive
> power of modern weapons, the danger of catastrophe will
> be imminent and probably at every moment everywhere.
> —Thomas Merton, *PFP*

In the last chapter I tried to present what I (and many others)
believe was Jesus' attitude toward people and toward relationships. In fact, there are some people who would maintain that
the nonviolence of Jesus was the moral stance of Christians for
at least the first three centuries of Christian existence—a stance
that underwent drastic modifications once Christians became
(especially after the time of Constantine) more involved in matters of state.

There was a time when I believed this was true of the early
Christian community (in fact I said as much in a book called
Seeking the Face of God). More recently I have come to the conclusion that such a position is at least open to question for a
number of reasons. In the first place, I would say that the nonviolence I talked about in the previous chapters involves a
sense of responsibility toward the world and its problems that
Christians *of today* might well be expected to have. It would be
their belief that followers of Jesus have a duty to do something
about violence, injustice, and inequality in our world. I am not
quite so sure that the *early* Christians would have had the same

kind of concern for the world of their time. Quite the contrary, they awaited a better world that would be inaugurated by the second coming of Christ. It was this new world that mattered. There was little reason to get involved in the affairs of this one, which was passing away.

In the second place, the understanding of nonviolence that I presented in the previous chapters involves not only an understanding of Jesus' teaching but also a new insight into the innate and equal dignity of each and every human person, no matter what his or her status or position in life might be. This insight into the equality of people simply as people exists in today's culture in a way it did not exist in the past. (This is what I meant when I spoke in chapter 8 of the dawning of a new consciousness.) Of course, this is not to say that today's society always acts out of that insight; but the insight is there, no matter how often it is violated.

But a culture—such as that into which Christianity first came to exist—that accepted slavery, the unquestioned inferiority of women, and the absolute rights of fathers over their children simply would not have been able to grasp the depths of meaning in the nonviolence of Jesus. Such an understanding had to await a belief in the equality and personal dignity of each and every human person and a realization of the need to act on that belief. This is why I say that today, because of the growth in human consciousness, we can plumb the depths of meaning of the nonviolence of Jesus in a way that was not possible for an earlier age in human history.

Finally, we live in an age wherein violence has taken on a new face. While it is true that violence has been destructive of human life and dignity in every age, it is only in our time (in the post-Hiroshima age) that we have achieved a point in the history of violence where violence has the power to destroy the world as we know it. The terrible face of nuclear violence has forced us to see the nonviolence of Jesus, based on the oneness of all humanity and expressed in unconditional love, as the only way to true security and wholesome peace. The alternative could be nuclear annihilation.

Early Christian Attitudes toward War

One way of discovering the stance of the early church toward violence is to look at the attitude of the early church toward war. Sweeping statements are sometimes made that the early church quite simply and unqualifiedly rejected any involvement in the military up to the time of Constantine in the fourth century. This is a thesis I would very much like to accept because of my own commitment to nonviolence and my personal conviction that nonviolence was the way of the Lord Jesus. But I think this position oversimplifies early church history and cannot be substantiated by the facts. I would prefer to put it this way. There is evidence, I believe, that up to the last part of the second century, the church was pacifist—that is, it refused to be involved in the military. From the time around A.D. 170, it becomes increasingly a fact that Christians were involved in the military.

What was the reason for pacifism in that early period of the church's life? There was a pluralistic approach to the question of bearing arms. One of the reasons for pacifism was the desire to imitate Jesus, but probably the most important reason was their hope for an imminent return of the Lord Jesus. The church, waiting for Christ's immediate return, saw itself in opposition to all that was worldly, including bearing arms. Thus, the early followers of Jesus accepted that Jesus' teaching called them to nonviolence, because they did not want to be involved in the world, which was so rapidly on its way out.

At this juncture I want, in a kind of parenthesis, to make a point I hope to come back to later: the difference between these early pacifists and pacifists today. The early pacifists rejected the military because they had little desire to get involved in the world in which they lived. Modern-day pacifists

(or if you don't like that term—today's men and women committed to nonviolence or conscientious objectors to war) are
rejecting war and military service not because they want to
escape from the world but precisely because they want to be
involved in their world. They refuse to abdicate to advocates of
war the power to make decisions that will affect their future,
the future of their children, and the future of the human race
as well as of the earth and its environment.

I think this distinction is very important: those of us who
believe today that Jesus calls us to a nonviolent life-style—which
necessarily must exclude involvement in military service—
refuse to take this understanding of Jesus' teaching as an
excuse to avoid assuming responsibilities in our world. On the
contrary, we are trying to live this understanding of Jesus'
teaching in such a way as to enable us to fulfill those responsibilities and thus to contribute to the well-being of all of
humanity and of the good earth God had given us.

In the period after A.D. 170 we do find soldiers in the Roman
army who are Christian. About the year A.D. 178 Celsus, a
pagan critic of Christianity, urged Christians to support the
emperor by taking part in civil government and also by serving
as soldiers. He argued that if everyone did as Christians were
doing, the emperor would be left alone and deserted and
earthly affairs would fall into the hands of lawless and savage
barbarians.

Tertullian

Tertullian, the first Christian writer to give extensive attention to the question of war, wrote in the year 197 to the
emperor Septimius Severus. In the *Apology*, while decrying the
killing and destruction that accompany war, Tertullian did not
deny that war may be necessary. He went on to tell the emperor
that Christians prayed for him and for brave armies as well. He
refuted the charge that Christians refused to enter the military.
He said that there were Christians in every camp and they
fought well; yet even in this *Apology* to the emperor, he
expressed his misgivings. As his other writings show, these mis-

givings were based to a great extent on the idolatrous practices that were part of life in the army. Hence, no Christian could remain in service after baptism.

An Unusual Roman Legion

Yet there is the story of the "Thundering Legion," (Legio XII Fulminata [*fulminata* = "thunderstruck," not "thundering"]) aiding Marcus Aurelius in A.D. 173. The legion was fighting the barbarians on the Danube frontier. It became trapped and was without food and water. The Christians in the legion prayed for deliverance. Immediately a rainstorm blew up that filled the Roman water barrels and sent down bolts of lightning on the enemy. All the Romans had to do was mop up.

This curious event, mentioned by Tertullian and in the *Church History* of Eusebius, suggests the stuff of legend. Yet it is attested to also by non-Christian sources, for example, Cassius Dio, a Roman historian who wrote in Greek an eighty-volume history of Rome from its beginning down to his own time. Perhaps even more significant is the fact that the event of the "Thunderstruck Legion" is depicted on the column of Marcus Aurelius in Rome. Whether the story of this unusual legion is true or not, it is significant that none of the several Christian writers who report it expressed any regret that Christians were involved in the victory. On the contrary, Tertullian, Eusebius, and others recount the incident with pride.

Origen

One of the most interesting Christian approaches to the subject of war was that of Origen (185–254)—one of the true giants of the early church. He, like Tertullian, answered Celsus (he wrote a whole treatise against him, the *Contra Celsum,* or *Against Celsus*). He said that although Celsus urged people to fight for the emperor, Christians could render more efficacious help by offering "prayers, intercessions, and supplications for the emperor." This was more effective than the work done by soldiers. Then he made an interesting point. He said to

Celsus: "You never enlist the priests in the army. . . . They keep their hands pure and wrestle in prayers to God on behalf of *those who are fighting in a righteous cause.* . . . So we by our prayers vanquish all demons who stir up war . . . and disturb the peace; in this way we are much more helpful to the kings than those who go into the field to fight for them" (*Against Celsus,* 8, 8.73).

According to Origen, (1) Christians are "priests"; therefore it is not proper for them (any more than it is for pagan priests) to fight with anything but spiritual arms. (2) Christians have an obligation to support those who are fighting in a "righteous cause"—but only in the way proper to priests. But still he does admit that their cause may be "righteous." This is the forerunner of the just-war attitude. (3) Christians are aiding the emperor in the most important way possible, for—Origen believed—once all the world became Christian, there would no longer be any need for force. [Origen was an idealist. History makes painfully clear that his ideal never became a reality in Christendom.]

Christian Influence in the Empire

Toward the end of the third century and into the fourth, Christians became more numerous and more influential in the empire. As their numbers grew, they became more identified with the interests and welfare of the empire, especially when the empire was being attacked by marauding peoples from the north. The link with the empire became practically indissoluble when Constantine (313–337) declared his support for Christianity, and especially when, under Theodosius (346–395) Christianity became the religion of the empire. The welfare of the church was increasingly identified with the defense of the Roman Empire.

Development of the Theory of the "Just War"

The Christian dilemma was this: the nonviolent teaching of Jesus is an essential element of the gospel. How could Christians adhere to that teaching and at the same time come to the defense of the empire? St. Ambrose, bishop of Milan (339–397), together with St. Augustine, bishop of Hippo (354–430), sought a way out of the dilemma. They found it by distinguishing between individual relationships and the social needs of the empire. As individuals, Christians should preserve nonviolence in their relationships with others; but as members of society, it was their responsibility to join in the defense of the empire when attacked by marauders from outside. Ambrose (who was perhaps more Roman than Christian—or, to put it more kindly, at least as Roman as he was Christian) was probably the first to make the equation: saving the empire = saving Christianity. Ambrose was the human instrument in Augustine's conversion to Christian Faith. He may also be seen as the inspiration behind Augustine's great work *The City of God*, which sees how the providence of God was involved in the coming into being of the Roman empire and the relationship of the Empire to Christianity.

In all fairness to Ambrose and Augustine, it should be pointed out that in the empire, where there were no sheriffs and police officers, the army very often carried out police duty, defending otherwise unprotected citizens from robbers, murderers, and other groups that were a threat to the personal safety of Roman citizens. Nevertheless, they did go to battle and kill. But Ambrose and Augustine made very clear that in going to war Christians could not cease to love their enemies. A curious way of expressing love though—thrusting a sword into the heart of the enemy and all the while loving him. Many people quote Augustine's well-known words: "Love and do what you will" in any number of contexts. They don't usually know the actual context of this remark. Augustine had been approached about the rightness of putting down the Donatist heresy by actually taking arms against them. Augustine gave his approval, but said that still they must love the Donatists: "Love them and then do what you will."

> *You are the enemy,*
> *So I must kill you,*

Though I don't even
Know your name.
But, I pray you, be
Consoled with this:
I love you
All the same.

Conditions for the Just War

Augustine's teaching of the "just war" became the common heritage of medieval theology, which specified, with increasing preciseness, the conditions necessary for such a war. Thomas Aquinas (1225–1274) expressed those conditions as clearly as anyone. He indicated three: (1) The war must be declared by competent authority (*auctoritas principis*), since it is the ruler's duty to defend the state as much against external enemies as against internal disturbers of the peace. (2) There must be a just cause (*causa justa*), which means that war is being waged because of some fault on the part of the enemy (*propter aliquam culpam*). (3) A right intention (*intentio bellantium recta*) is required on the part of those engaged in the war. This means that the wars must be waged for promoting good or avoiding evil. If there is a just cause for war, but no right intention—if for instance the motive is to harm the enemy or to seize power or wealth or if the war is fought with cruelty or out of a spirit of revenge—such a war would be immoral. The surest sign of a right intention is the sincere desire to achieve peace. And I need to ask: Must not a right intention also include love for the enemy? And is such love psychically possible when one is in battle? To ask this question is to call forth an even more shocking one: Can there be, has there ever been, a war that could be described as "just"?

Those who proposed the theory of the just war accepted the inevitability of wars. Their intent was to lay down principles that, as far as possible, would limit war and the havoc it necessarily spawned. There were other efforts made to diminish the terrible effects of war. The monastic orders, during the feudal period when there were many local wars, did their best to promote periods of peace where fighting would be forbidden. Thus, the famous "Truce of God," whereby people would abstain from war certain days of the week and certain seasons of the year.

The Emergence of National States and of the "Right" of War

From Justum Bellum to Ius ad Bellum

It is one thing to say that a war could be right (that is, just) but quite a different thing to say that war *is* a right. The sixteenth and seventeenth centuries saw a drastic rethinking of the theory of the "just war." Speculation moved from the "moral" sphere to the "juridical." The "just war" (*justum bellum*) became the "right of war" (*ius belli* or *ius ad bellum*). I use the Latin here to point out that *iustum* (the letters *i* and *j* are interchangeable in Latin) is pretty closely related to *ius*. "Just war" (*iustum bellum*) was transformed by canon lawyers into "right to war" (*ius belli*).

This was quite a transformation, since, as I have already pointed out, the "just war theory" was intended to restrict war as far as possible. It certainly was not developed to establish a right to wage war. What accounted for this dramatic change in perspective? It was the birth in the last centuries of the Middle Ages of the national or modern state, whose essential characteristic is its own sovereignty. Recognizing no power superior to itself, the modern state considers itself the sole judge of its own rights and interests and claims *the right to wage war* against another state if it judges its rights and interests to have been violated.

This made for a whole new "ball game," in which Roman Catholic theologians and jurists, such as the Spanish Dominican Francisco de Vitoria (ca. 1480–1546) and the Spanish Jesuit Francisco Suarez (1548–1617) were prominent participants. They accepted the principle of state sovereignty and saw that sovereignty as establishing a new right: one they had never even thought of before, namely, the "*right* to wage war."

A New Way of Thinking about the Just War

What this did was to create a subtle, but important, difference in the way in which the theory of the "just war" came to be applied. No longer was it used simply to determine the legitimacy or illegitimacy of a war. Now it would be used to determine whether a *right* was being carried out properly or not. *The presumption was no longer that war had to be justified.* War was now something a state was entitled to, a *right* it possessed, though the state had to exercise that right in an appropriate way. Theologians tried their best to use the theory of the "just war" to limit and control what was now recognized as a state's right.

Thus, according to Francisco de Vitoria, the right to wage war is justified only for one of three reasons: (1) to defend one's own possessions, (2) to punish another nation that has clearly violated one's rights and therefore is deserving of punishment, or (3) to defend oneself against an unjust aggressor.

To these three reasons that would justify exercising the right to wage war, F. de Vitoria added two correctives. The first is what we today would call the principle of proportionality: there must be a proportion between the gravity of the injustice that has been inflicted and the evil consequences that will result from war. The second corrective was that war for the advantage of a particular country would not be justified if such a war would cause harm to Christianity or to the whole world.

This second corrective might well be called (as we would call it today) the principle of totality. When F. de Vitoria spoke of causing harm to the whole world, it is not clear exactly what he had in mind. Certainly he could never have conceived of the kind of global destruction that a nuclear holocaust would produce.

The Nuclear Age

It was the first use of thermonuclear weapons that changed the very nature of war. Such weapons made *modern warfare* radically different from wars of the past. The date 6 August 1945 marks a decisive change in the history of humankind, for the dropping of the nuclear bomb on Hiroshima moved the world irrevocably into the period of "total warfare." With the highly sophisticated thermonuclear weapons that have emerged since 1945, the term "total warfare" takes on a meaning more sinister and terrifying than ever. If the Second World War became total through the carpet bombing of cities and therefore of civilian populations, with casualty lists of more than five million dead, how much more "total" will war be today! A war fought with thermonuclear weapons today could mean hundreds of thousands would die in the first hours; in fact, it could mean the destruction of every form of life over a large part of the planet earth.

The Editorial in La Civilta Cattolica

In July 1991, an editorial in *La Civilta Cattolica* (a Jesuit publication from Rome that carries special weight, because it is often used as a vehicle for "official" church statements) offered radically new reflections on the theory of the just war. These reflections were as revolutionary in their own way as the radical rethinking of the seventeenth-century jurists. The seventeenth-century writers expanded the meaning of "just war"; the editorial in *La Civilta* so minimized the possibility of just war as to practically eliminate it. It is a document so radical that, if accepted, it could move the Catholic Church in the direction of becoming a "peace church."

What did this editorial say? While it praises the worthy intentions of those who developed this theory (their desire was not to "justify" war, but to limit its frequency and brutality), the editorial declares unequivocally: "[This] theory has a serious flaw: its conditions are unattainable; a war cannot really be conducted according to the criteria required for a just war." Not only are the conditions unattainable now; they really never have been attainable, because, even when there may be a just cause, war *by its very nature* is waged with brutality. It always produces harm that far outweighs the advantages that may be achieved; it always goes beyond what is needed to win the war. For the proper "logic" of war is to so cripple the adversary that he will no longer pose any danger. These are strong words, asserting that there never has been a truly "just" war.

The Persian Gulf War of 1991, the editorial suggests, clearly illustrates this viewpoint. It began with a "just motive" (the liberation of Kuwait from the Iraqi invasion); it ended with the systematic destruction of Iraq. As many as ninety thousand tons of bombs (so it has been reported) were dropped on Iraq killing or wounding incalculable numbers of Iraqi civilians and destroying much of the Iraqi army. Thus the liberation of Kuwait caused the destruction of a country and the deaths of hundreds of thousands of people.

Given such a situation and the practical realization that another war would follow the same scenario, does it any longer make sense to speak of a "just war?"

> Or do we not rather have to say a "just war" is impossible because, even when a just cause is present, the wrongs that wars produce by their very nature are so grave and dreadful that they can never be justified in the light of conscience? (*La Civilta Cattolica*, 6 July 1991; see *Origins*, 19 December 1991)

This is all the more true, the editorial contends, because wars are neither necessary nor inevitable, since the wrongs they seek to redress can be rectified by other means that are no less effective than war. Some would justify war but only as a *last resort*. Yet war is never the last resort. For there are always peaceful means for resolving conflicts, provided one has the will to use them and the patience to give them time to work. It is so easy to declare that war has become the "last resort," when in reality one is using this as an excuse to justify a war that one wants to wage. Even the term "just cause" has to be carefully scrutinized: it can so easily be used as a moral and juridical cover-up for a war that one intends to wage for quite different reasons.

At one point the editorial *seems* to back away from this uncompromising condemnation of war. For it speaks of a single exception in which it might be possible to justify war, though it couches that exception in carefully chosen words: "a war of pure defense against an aggression actually taking place (*in presenza di un'aggressione in atto*)." It was deemed necessary, I suspect, to make mention of such an exception, since the "right of legitimate self-defense," at least in certain circumstances and in the absence of any international authority to deal with conflicts, was accepted by Pope Pius XII and by the Second Vatican Council.

But the editorial, while allowing such an exception in theory, moves rather quickly to suggest that today there is scarcely the slimmest possibility that a war begun in legitimate self-defense could *remain* just in its execution. The reason why the editorial denies in practice what it reluctantly admits in theory is that modern warfare *by its very nature* allows the use of weapons of mass destruction, which elude human control. This is true even of conventional weapons which have reached a point where they have enormous destructive power.

The advent of modern warfare, which almost inevitably tends toward total war, has, therefore, made even the war of legitimate defense morally questionable. Modern warfare, as distinguished from war in past ages, inevitably runs afoul of the principle of totality. In the past, war remained "local" and "partial." Today, however, it has increasingly become total—and that in a threefold sense, as the editorial suggests: "First it involves whole nations, entire populations, all the cultural, artistic and religious wealth and the economic riches of a country. Second, it involves not only two nations or a single group of nations, but many nations and ultimately the whole world. And, finally, it uses weapons of 'total' and 'indiscriminate' destruction which elude the possibility of human control."

It is significant that after discussing the "war of self- defense," and the moral shadows that modern warfare has shed even on this kind of war, the editorial ends with this exceptionless statement: "[W]e can only conclude that modern warfare is *always* immoral" (italics added).

Even if modern warfare were not immoral, it would have to be rejected for pragmatic reasons: it is useless and harmful. For it not only fails to solve the problems that occasion it; it actually aggravates those problems. Indeed, it often creates problems worse than those it was intended to resolve. Inevitably it sows the seeds of future conflicts and wars. The "peace" of Versailles which ended World War I planted the seed that grew into World War II. The Gulf War brought in its wake the destruction of Iraq and the economic ruin of Kuwait. Furthermore, there was the massacre of Palestinians (and Iraqis too) in Kuwait; the civil war in Iraq, which led to the slaughter of many Kurds and Shiites; the pollution of much of the Persian Gulf; not to mention the military cost of the war. Violence always begets more violence.

There is, moreover, the fact that none of the problems of the Middle East—the plight of the Palestinians, the Lebanese, and the Kurds—were resolved by the war. If anything, their solution was rendered more difficult. "Therefore it seems clear that this [Persian Gulf] war was not only immoral but also irrational, because it proved useless and produced further disasters."

The experience of the Gulf War helps us to understand why the church in the twentieth century has been moving away from past teaching about the just war and the holy war in defense of the faith and has increasingly adopted a position in which Christian conscience has come to see the "absolute immorality of war." Pope John Paul II sums up the development of the church's official teaching in the twentieth century in these moving words of his encyclical *Centesimus Annus:*

> No, never again war, which destroys the lives of innocent people, teaches how to kill, throws into upheaval even the lives of those who do the killing and leaves behind a trail of resentment and hatred, thus making it all the more difficult to find a just solution of the very problems which provoked the war.

Merton, War, and Contemplative Spirituality

It was contemplation that led Merton to the belief that he had to oppose war and, further, that it was his responsibility to encourage all peoples of good will to do the same. In contemplation he had experienced his own oneness with God and the oneness in God of all peoples and indeed of all reality. Violence—and especially the ultimate violence, war—obscures that oneness and makes us believe that it doesn't really exist. For a contemplative, then, war is the ultimate illusion: not in the sense that it doesn't exist but in the sense that it seeks to blind people to the most important fact of reality: the unity of humankind in God. War perpetuates, therefore, the ultimate illusion. It places us in a world of separateness and alienation— a world that in ultimate terms is not the real world at all. War is the ultimate symbol of the fall from paradise. The ultimate symbol of original sin. For the fall was the loss of paradise: the loss of harmony, the loss of awareness of reality as it is. War thrusts us into a state of ultimate illusion, for it strikes out against what is the very heart of all that is real: namely, the oneness of all reality in God. War is the denial of the contemplative vision of reality. That is why contemplation is necessarily a rejection of all war.

Peace Movement and the Catholic Church

Today the number of Catholics committed to nonviolence is increasing. Will the peace movement in the Catholic Church continue to grow? I believe it will. As more and more people develop the contemplative side of their nature, as more and more people see the futility of war, there will be a stronger movement in the direction of nonviolence and, as there was an emancipation proclamation against slavery a century ago, so there will be an emancipation proclamation against war.

Yet the peace movement is not yet at the center of Catholic moral teaching. For many it is still seen as very much of a minority position. In fact it might be said that the peace movement in the Roman Catholic Church today is in a situation similar to that of the liturgical movement in the decades before Vatican II. The liturgical movement comprised a zealous minority within the church pushing for liturgical renewal, but the movement was outside the mainstream of Catholic life and thought. The Second Vatican Council, with its sweeping liturgical reforms, changed all this: it placed the goals and directions of the liturgical movement at the heart of Catholic life and wor-

ship. In a somewhat similar way, the peace movement is a movement within the church that is very much alive today. This by
itself, however, does not make the Roman Catholic Church a
Christian peace church in the sense that other Christian
churches are "peace churches." That will happen only when the
Catholic Church embraces the peace movement, places the
movement's commitment at the center of the church's life
stream and thus makes it not just a movement *in* the church but
also a movement *of* the church.

CHAPTER ELEVEN

Is Nonviolence a Viable Possibility?

Non-violence is a flop. The only bigger flop is violence.
—Joan Baez, *21st Century Dictionary of Quotations*

The last chapter was a long [long-winded, you might want to say] discussion of the ultimate expression of violence which is war. I concluded it with the impassioned plea of Pope John Paul II for peace: a peace that would forever consign war to deep caverns of the tragic past of history. Yet even as I write this, and probably as you read it, there is war going on in so many places. Lives everywhere are being destroyed by violence—and not just by war. There is street violence, family violence, even violence people do to themselves.

It is becoming clear to an ever-increasing number of people that the only weapon that can stop the spiraling violence in our society is a total commitment to a life of nonviolence. Some may think that this is too idealistic, even naïve. There is a violent streak in human nature, people will say. It cannot be eradicated. The time will never come when there will be a sufficient number of people committed to a nonviolent life-style, so that they will be able to make a difference.

Perhaps it has to be said that history is on the side of those who would make such a statement. But, as I have been trying to suggest, I believe that we have reached a point in the development of human consciousness where an alternative to violent living can be viewed as a viable possibility. If history tells us that the human story has been one of conflict and violence, it

also makes clear that such conflict and violence has brought
misery and pain and oppression to men, women, and children.
As Joan Baez, the American folk-singer has said: "Non-violence
is a flop. The only bigger flop is violence."

If thus far nonviolence has proved to be a flop, the problem
may be that we have to do a better job of correcting misunder-
standings people have of it and of clarifying for them what
nonviolence is in its deepest meaning, how it operates, what it
can achieve, and why it is desperately needed today. We have to
explore its hidden potential. Most people have yet to discover
the tremendous power latent in nonviolence.

Let me offer a simple example of what I mean. At the
moment I am writing this text on a fairly powerful computer,
but I have to admit that I am borderline when it comes to computer literacy. This computer facing me could well say to me:
"You scarcely know me at all. I have the capability of doing all
sorts of things for you that you haven't even dreamed about. It
will take effort and discipline on your part, but it's worth your
while to get to know me. Once you do, you will be astounded at
what I can accomplish for you." I know this is true. I have
turned this computer into a glorified typewriter, and its skill to
do all sorts of other things for me is waiting there for me to
discover.

You may remember that in the introduction I created an
imaginative picture of Nonviolence being given the opportunity to speak to us. What I had my computer say to me just a
moment ago, Nonviolence could say to all of us. It is a power
for justice and peace whose depths we haven't even begun to
plumb. Nonviolence is not just an approach to war. It's not just
an alternative to violence. It is a way of life that must affect
everything we do. Let me put it this way: the conclusion that
war is wrong is but one of a whole trajectory of conclusions,
options, and directions that begin to emerge when persons
start living their lives in a totally nonviolent way. Nonviolence
does not exist simply to declare war wrong; it exists to declare
that unconditional love is always and everywhere right. A nonviolent stance in life calls me to commit myself ever more fully

to that kind of love. And I need to reiterate the point that such a commitment finds its roots in the contemplative vision. We—women, men, relatives, friends, lovers, enemies—are one in God. Sadly, we don't always advert to that oneness, but in faith we know it is there and in times of deep spiritual perception we experience it. The call of nonviolence is to live this oneness at all times. As my computer waits for me to discover the wondrous things it can accomplish for me, so nonviolence awaits the day when we shall discover at last the potential for peace, justice, and general well-being that it can generate in human society. We must not keep it waiting too long.

Malcolm X once said: "Non-violence is fine as long as it works." This is a faulty understanding that robs nonviolence of its power. Nonviolence is not just a choice we make on occasion. It must be there at all times. It is not an attitude we adopt simply when it is advantageous to us to do so. It has to become a habit, a kind of second nature to us. It must be a total commitment. I would like to spend most of this chapter discussing with the reader some of the commitments involved in a nonviolent life-style. But before doing that let's look at the word itself. Where did it come from and what is its deepest meaning?

Nonviolence: A Relatively New Word

The first thing we can say about the word "nonviolence" is that, as language goes, it is quite new. It's a twentieth-century word. The huge *Oxford English Dictionary* dates its first use as 1922 and the first user Mohandas Gandhi. The dictionary is giving the earliest date of its known appearance in print. But Gandhi used it earlier than that, as I shall point out in a moment. Meanwhile listen to the *OED*'s definition of "nonviolence": "the principle or practice of abstaining from the use of violence." This might be called a generic definition, strictly etymological. You will notice that it seems clearly to suggest an attitude or approach that is quite negative: not doing something. A definition of this sort misses the point of nonviolence. For nonviolence, as Gandhi understood it, very definitely means doing something. But it is doing based on being. Let me try to clarify.

Nonviolence is the English equivalent of a Sanskrit word that was important to Gandhi: *ahimsa.* The word is made up of *himsa,* which means "injury," and the prefix *a-.* Since *a-* (alpha privative) negates what follows it, the literal translation of *ahimsa* turns out to be "noninjury" or "nonviolence." And that surely sounds pretty negative. The problem—one that a translator must frequently face—is that a literal, purely etymological translation of a word may not convey is true and deepest meaning. For words do not exist in a vacuum: they tend to pick up meanings not discoverable in their etymological roots. Translating *ahimsa* literally misses the *positive* significance the word has taken on in the Indian mind. *Ahimsa* has assimilated into itself the philosophical reason in Indian thought for not doing injury to another. That reason is the oneness of all reality. To use *ahimsa* and ignore the cultural accretions it has picked up is to falsify what it really means.

Satyagraha

In the years he was working to better the social and economic conditions of Indians in South Africa, Gandhi anglicized *ahimsa* into "civil disobedience"—a term borrowed from Henry Thoreau, or more often "passive resistance." But he was not satisfied with either. In 1906, in a magazine called *Indian Opinion,* which he edited for a time in South Africa, he offered a small prize to be "awarded to the reader who invented the best designation for our struggle." One of his cousins, Maganlal Gandhi, produced a word that seemed almost right, *sadagraha,* which means "firmness in a good cause." Gandhi corrected it to *satyagraha.* [Does that mean he awarded the mysterious prize to himself?] *Satya* means "Truth"; *graha* means "firmness, tenacity, holding on." "I thus began," Gandhi says, "to call the Indian movement *satyagraha,* that is to say the Force that is born of truth and love, or non-violence," and gave up the use of the phrase "passive resistance." On other occasions Gandhi called it "Soul-Force," or "Love-Force," or "Truth-Force." *Sat* in *satyagraha* means "being," "that which is," "truth." For Gandhi, *Sat* was "the only correct and fully significant name for God" (M. K. Gandhi, *Non-Violent Resistance*). [Note the contemplative intuition that is so obviously embedded in Gandhi's thought.]

As far as I know, no one has found an English equivalent for *satyagraha.* Hence, we are still obliged to content ourselves with the word "nonviolence." But we need continually to make clear the positive meaning it intends to convey as a translation of *ahimsa.*

Those who live *satyagraha* are called *satyagrahi(s).* Though these words have found their way into English dictionaries, they have not found their way into common usage. So you might get some strange looks from people if you told them: "I'm a *satyagrahi."* Indeed, nonviolence is so misunderstood that you might even get strange looks if you said: "I am committed to nonviolence" especially if you said: "I am committed to it at all times and in every situation, no matter what it is."

The Commitments
to Which Nonviolence Calls Us

At this point, I would like to return to the kind of commitments involved in being a *satyagrahi,* in making the choice of a nonviolent style of life. As I write about these commitments, I am painfully aware how easy it is to outline them in writing. One could even do so with fervor and enthusiasm. Putting them on paper isn't difficult at all. It's living them that's hard. For nonviolence can make bothersome, disagreeable, sometimes even heroic, demands of us. The choice to live a nonviolent life-style is not one that a sensible person makes lightly.

Commitment to the Truth

The first commitment of a nonviolent person is to the truth. Gandhi, quoted by Merton, sums up the heart of his teaching about non-violence: "The way of peace is the way of truth." He even says: "Truthfulness is more important than peacefulness. Indeed, *lying is the mother of violence. A* truthful person cannot long remain violent" (*CGB*, 84). Gandhi offers his reason for saying this: "A person will perceive in the course of his research that he has no need to be violent, and he will further discover that so long as there is the slightest trace of violence in him, he will fail to find the truth he is searching for." At the deepest level of our being we are in touch with God and therefore with truth itself. That is why at the core of our being we are nonviolent. And that is why I keep insisting on the link with contemplation. Contemplation is discovering the depths of our being. It is therefore the discovery of God and of Truth and of Nonviolence.

In his essay "Blessed Are the Meek," Merton warns us that the nonviolent person is not fighting for "his truth" or for the right that is "on his side." "On the contrary, both his strength and his weakness come from the fact that he is fighting for *the* truth, common to him and to the adversary, *the* right which is objective and universal. He is fighting for *everybody*" (*PFP*, 249). That is why, Merton points out, Gandhi saw that "the fully consistent practice of nonviolence demands a solid metaphysical and religious basis both in being and in God. This comes *before* subjective good intentions and sincerity" (ibid.). A Hindu such as Gandhi would express that basis in one way; a Christian such as Merton in another way. But that basis must be there.

For the Hindu, as Merton writes, "this metaphysical basis [is] provided by the Vedantist doctrine of the Atman, the true transcendent Self which alone is absolutely real and before which the empirical self of the individual must be effaced in the faithful practice of *dharma* [the duties proper to one's state of life]" (*PFP*, 249–50).

For the Christian, Merton says, "the basis of non-violence is the Gospel message of salvation for all men and the Kingdom of God to which *all* are summoned." If all are called, then my love must extend to all. There can be no true nonviolence that is not inclusive. The distinguished theologian Karl Barth, who was forced to flee Hitler's Germany, was once asked: "What would you say to Hitler, if you were to meet him?" Barth's answer, in the purest tradition of the Gospel and of nonviolence, was simply this: "I would say to him: 'Christ died to save you from your sins.'"

Respect for the Dignity of Every Person

Nonviolence always means a deep respect for the inherent dignity of the human person. This flows from the understanding of *ahimsa,* which teaches us the essential oneness of all reality. [Note again a contemplative insight.]

Merton makes the point that nonviolent persons refuse to see the struggle as based on the division between us, "the good guys," and those others—the wicked, the unenlightened, the communists, the capitalists, the racists, and so on. Thus, he writes: "Christian nonviolence is not built on a presupposed division, but on the basic unity of man. It is not out for the conversion of the wicked to the ideas of the good, but for the healing and reconciliation of man with himself, man the person and man the human family" (ibid.).

Nonviolence, to put it another way, seeks to develop and enrich human life, not to maim it or destroy it. This means that it is directed against existent evil rather than against the persons who may be doing the evil. Martin Luther King, Jr., said to the people of Montgomery:

> The tension in this city is not between white people and Negro people. The tension is, at bottom, between justice and injustice, between the forces of light and the forces of darkness. And if there is a victory, it will be a victory not merely for fifty thousand Negroes, but a victory for justice and for the forces of light. We are out to defeat injustice and not white persons who may be unjust. (*Stride toward Freedom,* 84)

Nonviolent Resistance to Evil

A third commitment is to confront violence wherever it exists. The nonviolent person accepts the obligation to resist evil: a point that is missed by those who see nonviolence as a sign of weakness. As a matter of fact, nonviolence is a way for the strong, not for the weak or cowardly. For it refuses to accept passively the presence of evil. It must oppose evil. This must be made clear. In fact, Gandhi said that, if cowardice were the only alternative to violence, it would be better to fight. Yet in the very saying of this Gandhi was well aware that there always is another alternative. An individual or a group does not have to submit to aggression and they do not have to respond with violence. There is always the way of nonviolent resistance—which is the way of the strong person.

Morally speaking, I do not have the choice to resist evil or not to resist. But I do have the choice of the way in which I will resist. Nonviolence is as active as violence in resisting evil; but it is a more creative way and, in the long run, a more effective way. Violence uses physical means to try to achieve a *win over the opponent* in order to crush the opponent. Nonviolence uses moral persuasion and spiritual energy to *win the opponent over,* so that he/she is no longer an opponent.

This means that the nonviolent person is not out to humiliate or defeat the opponent; rather her/his intent is to establish mutual understanding and friendship that will be beneficial to both. An important principle of nonviolence, then, is that one must always resist evil, but in a nonviolent way.

Freeing the Oppressor

A nonviolent person commits him-/herself to the goal of liberating not only the oppressed but the oppressor. This means that a person who lives nonviolence believes that human persons are capable of changing, that they have consciences that can be appealed to. We tend to label people and then, having pigeonholed them, we refuse to think they can become other. Whereas the way of violence inevitably brings out the worst in people, *nonviolence seeks to bring out the best in people.* This means that you have to believe that the possibility of that best is present in them.

Nonviolence, therefore, seeks the salvation and redemption of the opponent, not his humiliation and defeat. As Merton puts it: "It strives to operate without hatred, without hostility, and without resentment. It works without aggression, taking the side of the good that it is able to find already present in the adversary" (*CGB*, 86). Merton points out that this is no easy thing to do. He suggests that we must be careful about the way in which we talk about our opponents. We have to be even more careful how we regulate our differences with our collaborators. Sometimes the most bitter arguments and the most virulent hatreds can arise among those who are supposed to be working for the same noble cause (e.g., the different ways good people can take about the best way to act in opposing abortion).

Need for Self-Criticism

A nonviolent person must be committed to self-purification of mind and heart. We have to examine carefully both our *possession* of the truth and our *fidelity* to it. We must realize that we are fallible human beings, that we can make mistakes. We do not possess all the truth. Hence, we must have an open ear to listen to the truth that the other person may have that we need to discover. The willingness to enter into dialogue is of great importance.

We also must examine our *fidelity* to the truth. Sometimes we ourselves are violent, because we are divided by the inner violence of our own infidelity to the truth. Thomas Merton often warned people in the peace movement of the need to rid themselves of the hidden aggressions that so often are present in us and go unnoticed, because we feel so sure of the rightness of our position. We have to empty ourselves of ill will and hostility toward the oppressor. We must refrain not only from injuring the oppressor but also from hating him/her. Martin Luther King, Jr., quotes Booker T. Washington as saying: "Let no one pull you so low as to make you hate him" (*Stride toward Freedom,*

106). This brings us to the heart of the matter. The other side of nonviolence is love. What we are speaking about, of course, is not a sentimental love, much less an affection for the oppressor. It is a love that comes from within and goes out to the other, not because of a lovableness in that person's actions but because one sees a human dignity, the very image of God, that even violence and evil cannot erase. It is the love that Jesus spoke of when he called his followers to love, not only the neighbor but the enemy and those who persecute them. Such love involves a strong understanding that can see beneath the surface of things and a redemptive good will that is willing to suffer for the well-being of other human beings. It is a love that looks not for the lovableness of the other but for his or her *need*, especially the need to be humanized.

Suffering and Nonviolence

Commitment to nonviolence inevitably implies the cross. It must involve a willingness to accept suffering, without retaliating in kind, to endure violence without ever inflicting it. "Rivers of blood may have to flow before we gain our freedom," Gandhi once said to the people of India, "but it must be our blood."

Martin Luther King, Jr., learned the hard way that nonviolence and suffering are yoked together. In April 1960 the *Christian Century* invited him to write about suffering and faith. In a brief article he detailed some of the ordeals he had been through: five times jailed, twice having his house bombed, and once being a victim of a near-fatal stabbing. "As my sufferings mounted," he wrote, "I soon realized there were two ways I could respond to my situation: either to react with bitterness or seek to transform the suffering into a creative force." He chose the second course. "I have attempted to see my personal ordeals as an opportunity to transform myself and heal the people involved in the tragic situation which now obtains. I have lived these last few years with the conviction that unearned suffering is redemptive." Like the apostle Paul, he could say humbly, but proudly: "I bear in my body the marks of the Lord Jesus."

Thomas Merton was once asked: "You believe in non-violence. Why don't you, as sign of protest against the war policies of your country, pour gasoline over your body and immolate yourself?" According to the story [I have heard this story, but do not know its source and, therefore, cannot vouch for its authenticity], Merton's answer was: "Because it would hurt!" I am sure he had deeper reasons than that. I believe he would have seen such an act as one of violence, and that would be his primary reason for not doing it. The story does show, however, his realization that nonviolence does demand suffering. One must never unreasonably seek it, but must be prepared to accept it when it comes. Merton's staunch opposition to war—at a time when he was practically the only well-known Catholic priest taking such a stance—caused him a great deal of anguish and self-doubt. His stance on war brought immense suffering to him. [For details, see *Passion for Peace.*]

Nonviolent Action and Results

Witnessing to the truth must be given a higher priority than the achieving of results. This does not mean that the nonviolent person is indifferent to the results, as if the results of one's actions did not matter. It means that the primary motivation is commitment to the truth and the conviction that ultimately—even though one may not see it—it will be the truth that will triumph.

In 1966 James Forest, a young peace activist connected with the *Catholic Worker,* wrote to Thomas Merton. He was feeling bleak and depressed: the peace movement seemed to be getting nowhere. Merton wrote that he quite understood his sense of desperation. He offered this advice:

Do not depend on the hope of results. When you are doing the sort of work you have taken on . . . you may have to face the fact that your work will be apparently worthless, and even achieve no result at all, if not perhaps results opposite to what you expect. As you get used to this idea you start more and more to concentrate not on the results, but on the value, the rightness, the truth of the work itself. And there too a great deal has to be gone through, as gradually you struggle less and less for an idea and more and more for specific people. . . . In the end it is the reality of personal relationships that saves everything. (*HGL*, 294)

Nonviolent Strategies

How does one translate nonviolent commitments into nonviolent action? Much depends on the kind of violence we are dealing with. Are we talking about conflicts that may exist between individuals ("micro-violence") or situations of violence that may be systemic in nature ("macro-violence")? When I speak of situations of systemic violence, I include any type of violence that is built into the very structures of a system (whether that system be the laws of a country, the oppressive operations of corporations, especially multinational corporations, or the structures of a particular institution, for example, a church).

Dealing with systemic violence is a wide and multifaceted issue in which the power of nonviolence must confront the political, social, economic powers that oppress and enslave people. It is the struggle to break down barriers that prevent cooperation, to change government policies (e.g., the civil rights movement in the United States) to frustrate invaders (e.g., the Danish nonviolent resistance to Nazi occupation troops), to paralyze empires and dictatorships (e.g., the nonviolent revolution against the Marcos government in the Philippines).

Discussing this area of nonviolence would require a volume or two of its own. Gene Sharp, in his three-volume work *The Politics of Non-Violent Action,* discusses 198 methods of nonviolent action, such as nonviolent protest and persuasion, noncooperation (social, economic, political) and nonviolent intervention. Apart from the fact that a detailed discussion of such matters would push this book beyond reasonable bounds of space, there is the more significant fact that I can claim no expertise in this area.

I would make just one observation. In dealing with systemic violence, the question has to be asked: *What enables a particular instance of violence to exist?* Usually the answer is that it has come about and continues to exist because it is supported by various forces. There is a certain *precariousness* about violence. It may be likened to a pyramid turned upside down and standing on its point. The only way a pyramid can stand on its point without falling is to have it held up and supported by various pillars. The first step in nonviolent action, then, is to identify the pillars that support a particular instance of violence.

Hildegard Goss-Mayr offers a similar analogy for looking at violence. She says:

> All situations of injustice and violence . . . are like spinning tops; if nobody gives the energy needed to make them turn and stand upright, they fall over. It is very important to draw up an inventory of all the sources of energy which keep a situation of violence going. We cannot allow ourselves not to analyze these forces very clearly, for they can also change and become the driving force of justice and peace. (*A Non-Violent Lifestyle*, 102)

She offers an example that occurred in the early 1960s when she and her husband Jean were in Brazil working with nonviolent groups. In São Paulo nine hundred workers at a cement factory went on strike for decent working conditions and decent wages. They realized that one of the forces supporting the unjust system that reduced them to poverty was the church. Yet they had sufficient faith in the humanness of their bishops that if they knew the truth they would withdraw their support. Their testimony moved thirty-five bishops to sign a petition in their favor addressed to the president of the company. The workers realized also that another powerful force against them was the media. For the journalists, the matter was simple: strikers meant communists, so they denounced the strikers. With the help of their lawyer, Mario de Jesus, they tackled the press. Eventually the truth about the strike was published in the largest São Paulo daily, *O Estado de São Paulo*. There was a change in public opinion and eventually the strikers achieved the rights they were working for.

This is but one instance illustrating the truth that violence cannot stand by itself. When the pillars supporting it are removed, it collapses. Systemic violence can be overcome. But it takes patience, persistence, commitment, and the willingness to suffer if necessary. The growth of groups like the Fellowship of Reconciliation and Pax Christi, as well as other similar groups, is an encouraging sign that more and more people refuse to accept the inevitability of violence in human society. They are convinced that today is "the seedtime of peace."

For some people nonviolence is so important to the way they desire to lead their lives that they have expressed their commitment in a vow. For those who might be drawn toward making such a vow, I offer as a possible form of such a vow the one drafted by Pax Christi, USA. It goes without saying that making a vow of this kind is a serious matter and should not be undertaken without a good deal of prayer and reflection. Probably it ought to be made, initially at least, for one year (in fact, this is included in the Pax Christi vow). Then one could decide whether or not to make a longer or even a lifetime commitment.

Vow of Nonviolence

Recognizing the violence in my own heart, yet trusting in the goodness and mercy of God, I vow for one year to practice the non-violence of Jesus who taught us in the Sermon on the Mount:

Blessed are the peacemakers, for they shall be called the sons and daughters of God. . . . You have learned how it was said: "You must love your neighbor and hate your enemy," but I say to you: Love your enemies, and pray for those who persecute you. In this way you will be daughters and sons of your Creator in heaven.

Before God the Creator and the Sanctifying Spirit, I vow to carry out in my life the love and example of Jesus

by striving for peace within myself and seeking to be a peacemaker in my daily life;

by accepting suffering rather than inflicting it;
by refusing to retaliate in the face of provocation and violence;
by persevering in nonviolence of tongue and heart;
by living conscientiously and simply so that I do not deprive others of the means to live;
by actively resisting evil and working nonviolently to abolish war and the causes of war from my own heart and from the face of the earth.

God, I trust in your sustaining love and believe that just as you gave me the grace and desire to offer this, so you will also bestow abundant grace to fulfill it.
(reproduced with the permission of Pax Christi USA, 348 East 10th St., Erie, PA 16503)

The Vow and the Gospel

I suppose that, as they read this vow, different readers will see different parts of it that would prove especially difficult for them to carry out. May I invite you to reflection: Which poses the greatest problem for you? Is it perhaps "accepting suffering rather than inflicting it"? Or maybe "refusing to retaliate in the face of provocation and violence"? I own up to the fact that the one that bothers me most (perhaps you also?) is that part of the vow that calls me to live simply so that I do not deprive others of the means to live. It was St. Elizabeth Anne Seton, I believe, who put it this way: "Live simply so that others may simply live." There are areas of my life wherein I would have to raise questions about the simplicity of my lifestyle. I refrain from being more specific lest my own self-image suffer from making too much confession in this book.

The vow of nonviolence is demanding indeed; and, as I have already suggested, one should take serious thought before making it. Yet if you reflect on it carefully, does it really demand anything more than what the Gospel of Jesus Christ already asks of us?

CHAPTER TWELVE

Nonviolence and St. Paul's Hymn to Love

𝕲

Agape is the love of God operating in the human heart. When we rise to love on the agape level, we rise to the position of loving the person who does the evil deed, while hating the deed which the person does.

—Martin Luther King, Jr., *A Testament of Hope*

A cartoon in a recent issue of the *New Yorker* attracted my attention. It showed a highway sign that read: "Exit 21. Last Exit before Exit 22." An obvious statement of the obvious, if there ever was one. Yet it expresses an important truth: once you pass exit 21, you will, in the normal course of events, end up at exit 22. If you don't want to get to exit 22, you had better get off at exit 21. In the last chapter I spoke of the commitments that persons must make if they choose to live a life-style that is nonviolent. Making such a choice may seem to place one at exit 22. By that I mean it seems to be a "catch-22 situation," namely, a situation where the commitments seem so demanding as to appear virtually impossible. You may be inclined to say: "This is too much for me. Let me off at exit 21, please. Exit 22 is a catch-22 connection. It calls for the impossible. It's not for me."

If that is your reaction, you are probably right in feeling this way. I am reminded of chapter 68 of the Rule of St. Benedict, which deals with a circumstance in which a monk is asked by his abbot to do something that is impossible. Benedict says that, in such a case, the monk should make his concerns known

to the abbot. If, however, the abbot still insists, then he should
go and do it anyway! Jesus calls us to a nonviolent, unconditional, all-inclusive love. We might well be inclined to say: "I
can't do that. It's impossible." Jesus' response is simple: "Do it
anyway." But to this he would also add what he said to St. Paul,
when Paul asked to be delivered from what seemed to him an
impossible situation: "My grace is sufficient for you, for power
is made perfect in weakness" (2 Corinthians 12:9). We *can* get
to exit 22 without its becoming a catch-22 connection—but only
through the grace of God.

In this chapter I want to discuss some of the qualities we
need to cultivate, with the help of God's grace, that will enable
us to be faithful to the commitments of nonviolence. I would
like to sketch the portrait of an ideal to strive for rather than a
goal one should expect to achieve right off. We all know, most
of us at least, that the Cain streak dies hard in us. We have to be
continually on the alert for signs of violence creeping, almost
unnoticed, into our lives. We have to make sure that we don't
get scared at exit 21 and decide to get off there.

Paul's Hymn to Nonviolence

It occurred to me that, since nonviolence is the flip side of
unconditional love, we might get some insights into the qualities that must go into the making of this portrait of the nonviolent person by looking at St. Paul's marvelous hymn about love
in the thirteenth chapter of First Corinthians. In this hymn
Paul uses one of three Greek words that may be translated as
"love." He does not use *eros,* which means an attraction toward
that which is beautiful or lovable. *Eros* is aesthetic love or
romantic love. It is love in which I seek primarily *my own personal benefit,* my own happiness or pleasure. Neither does Paul
use the word *philia,* which is the love that friends have for one
another. The love of friendship looks for *mutual benefit.* It seeks
the happiness and well-being of both parties to the friendship.

The Greek word that Paul does use is *agape. Agape* is love that

seeks to *benefit the other*, whether that other be friend or enemy.
If *eros* is *self-centered* and *philia friend-centered*, *agape* is *other-cen-tered*. Disinterested and unselfish, it is redeeming love and good
will that reach out to both friend and foe. It refuses to distin-
guish between those who deserve our love and those who
don't. For it sees in every one the dignity of a human person
and the image of God. *Agape* might well be seen as the Greek
equivalent of the Sanskrit *ahimsa*. "Agapeic" love and "ahim-
saic" noninjury are both rooted in the contemplative intuition
of our oneness with one another in the Divine.

Love, it is often said, is blind. That may be true of *eros*, even
perhaps (though less likely) of *philia*—but never of *agape*. *Agape*
is preeminently the love that sees. It sees the good in others
that most people cannot see. For *agape* is nothing less than
God's love shared with us, which enables us to see others
through God's eyes, as it were, and love with God's love. In the
First Epistle of John we read: "We love because God first loved
us"(4:19). This passage does not specify the object of love. It
does not say we love someone; it simply states that we love (i.e.,
are able to love) because God first loved us.

To return to Paul's hymn on love, let us read it, but substitute
"nonviolence" for "love." We can then reflect briefly on the
descriptive adjectives or adjectival phrases Paul uses to identify
"love" (i.e., nonviolence).

> If I speak in the tongues of mortals and of angels,
> but fail in nonviolence,
> I am a noisy gong or a clanging cymbal.
> And if I have prophetic powers
> and understand all mysteries and all knowledge
> and if I have all faith, so as to remove mountains,
> but fail in nonviolence, I am nothing.
> If I give away all my possessions
> and if I hand over my body so that I may boast
> but fail in nonviolence, I gain nothing.
> Nonviolence is patient;
> Nonviolence is kind;
> Nonviolence is not envious or boastful

or arrogant or rude.
It does not insist on its own way;
It is not irritable or resentful;
it does not rejoice in wrong-doing,
but rejoices in the truth.
It bears all things,
believes all things,
hopes all things,
endures all things. . . .
                    (1 Corinthians 13:1–7, adapted from NRSV)

The Qualities of a Nonviolent Life-Style

Nonviolence is patient. The word "patient" is actually a participle from the Latin verb *patior,* whose literal meaning is "to suffer, to endure, to put up with something." If you're into Greek, the word Paul uses is *makrothymei,* which means "restraining *thymos,* or anger. It is somewhat akin to the Sanskrit word used by Gandhi, *ahimsa,* which, you will remember, means "noninjury.

We sometimes use "patient" as a noun, designating someone who visits, say, a doctor or a dentist. Unless our visit is purely social, it is not something we ordinarily look forward to or anticipate as a pleasant experience. It's something we "put up with" when our body needs attention. More often, we use "patient" as an adjective. When we speak of a "patient person," we usually have in mind someone who is willing to put up with a disagreeable situation and is still able to preserve a calmness of spirit. A person who sits in his or her car in a traffic jam, where no cars move for half an hour, and who remains calm and unruffled (not even tooting his or her horn!), would be deserving, we would probably say, of some sort of award as "the most patient person of the year."

Our patience is tried in many situations. Very often it may simply be a circumstance in which we are obliged to wait longer than we think we ought, say in a supermarket line, waiting—

when you finally are next at the register—for the person ahead of you to lay out his/her seemingly countless coupons in partial payment of the bill. Or it may be waiting at a busy signal on your phone when you need to get in touch with someone quickly or waiting for a late guest to arrive for a dinner that is already getting cold. Many and diverse situations can put our patience to the test. How well do we face these sorts of tests? The answer will serve as one of a number of ways of evaluating our progress toward a nonviolent life-style.

Nonviolence is kind. A kind person is one who has a gentle, sympathetic, benevolent disposition. He or she sees the good side of people and wants to help them when they are in need. The Greek word Paul uses (*kreistos*) implies a readiness to be of service to others, without concern or thought of a return for that kindness. It is in this sense that Luke uses the same word when he says: "[God] is *kind* to the grateful and the wicked" (6:35). These words appear in that very special verse which is one of the "classic texts" for nonviolence. It is the verse in which Jesus commands us: "Love your enemies, do good and lend, expecting nothing in return." Then he goes on to describe, for our imitation, God's "kindness" to the ungrateful and the wicked. Once again we're challenged to the seemingly impossible task of being like our God. Kindness as God is kind must, therefore, be a significant part of the portrait we are sketching of the nonviolent person.

Nonviolence is not envious or boastful. The word Paul employs for "envious" [you have probably had your fill of Greek words, so I won't bother putting them in any more] in its original sense has a positive meaning: "zeal" for some laudable cause. It especially means "zeal" for God's glory. Here, however, it doesn't have that sort of meaning; for it signifies a jealous guarding of one's own status and position, which manifests itself in an envy at the prosperity and good fortune of others. It is a small-mindedness that refuses to be happy about the blessings that may come to others. "How come he got an A+ and I only got a B?" "Why did she get that promotion when I so obviously deserved it?"

It is sad that when blessings come to others, they are looked upon as a threat to one's own position. How much better it would be if we could say: "Congratulations for getting the A+. You deserved it. As for me I'm lucky I got the B. I was afraid it might be a C+." "Best wishes on your promotion. No one deserved it more than you." [I am assuming of course that these latter statements do embody the truth. There are times when people get honors they don't really deserve. A nonviolent person is never called to make people feel good by lying to them.]

A person without envy is genuinely solicitous to pursue the welfare and happiness of others. Such a person is not *boastful.* They are not so wrapped up in the pursuit of their own self-interest that they want everyone to know and appreciate their own good qualities; nor do they ever exaggerate their gifts, as the boastful do, in order to receive admiration and popularity. Envy and boastfulness can be no part of nonviolence, because both amount to trifling with the truth.

Nonviolence is not arrogant or rude. The Greek word for "arrogant" I found rather picturesque. It suggests a pair of bellows consisting of air chambers that expand or contract as air is forced through a nozzle. "Arrogance" is the "expanded" stage, where one is puffed up [pumped up] with his or her own sense of pride, conceit, and exaggerated self-importance. How incompatible with nonviolence, which always involves a commitment to the truth! Equally incompatible with nonviolence is *"rudeness."* To be "rude" is to act in a way that is rough, harsh, and unbecoming. Such actions, especially if they become habitual, belie any belief one might profess in the equal dignity of every human person.

Nonviolence does not insist on its own way. It seeks to resolve problem situations neither by insisting that its own approach is always right nor by simply yielding to the demands of the other. Instead it searches for a way that will do justice to both sides. This implies a willingness to enter into dialogue: to share one's own insights and to listen to the insights of the other. This is a very demanding piece of the nonviolent picture; for it so often happens that we are so convinced of the rightness of our own position that it is difficult to understand how anyone could have such poor sense as to think differently from us.

Nonviolence is not irritable. The literal meaning of the text is: "it does not allow itself to be provoked." Remember that Paul was writing these words to the Corinthian church where there were a good many tensions and a good many people (it seems) easily provoked into violence. Being provoked blinds our vision: we so easily lose sight of the true issues that are at stake; we tend to cloud the situation instead of clearing the air.

Nonviolence is not resentful. The literal meaning of the Greek word is that the nonviolent person is not someone who keeps a record, an account, of what has been done to him or her. Resentment carries with it the notion of "getting even," of "keeping score," and then "evening the score." Resentment suggests retaliation, which—as I have already pointed out—is rejected by Jesus as a way of settling differences.

Nonviolence does not rejoice in wrongdoing but rejoices in the truth. "Wrongdoing" is action that undermines the truth. It puts the truth in jeopardy. Thus it is opposed to the most fundamental commitment of nonviolence, namely, its commitment to the truth. Nonviolence must always rejoice when the truth is done and when truthfulness is manifested.

So, my friend, you might want to reflect on the other things Paul says about *agape* (nonviolence), but the above is a partial portrait of what you and I ought to look like, if we really believe that nonviolence is the only way for us to go. It's a "catch-22" situation, if there ever was one—except of course for Jesus' promise that he would be with us and that his grace would be sufficient for us.

The Beginning of Reality

ℊ

> I believe that one day humankind will bow before the altars
> of God and be crowned triumphant over war and blood-
> shed, and non-violent redemptive good will will be pro-
> claimed the rule of the land.
> —Martin Luther King, Jr., *A Testament of Hope*

If you have managed to persevere to this point in your reading of this book, it will be clear to you, at least I hope it will be,
that my intent has been to present three basic theses:

(1) The foundational truth of Christian faith is belief in the
reality of the resurrection of Jesus. The central Christian
proclamation is: God raised Jesus from the dead. Presumably
this made sense to you or you would not have proceeded
beyond the introduction.

(2) Closely related to that foundational truth are the two
themes that are the topic of this book: (a) our communion with
one another in God (which contemplation is all about) and (b)
the unconditional love we must show to one another and to all
God's people (which can only be achieved in a context of nonviolence).

(3) Contemplation and nonviolence are intimately related to
each other. They cannot exist separately. A violent person cannot be contemplative. Contemplation inevitably leads a person
to a nonviolent life-style.

I want to bring this book to a conclusion on a note of hope
and anticipation of a brighter future. Despite the many

catastrophes and disasters we face in a world of terrible violence and meaningless destructiveness, important forces are in
motion that will be the catalysts for dramatic and, I believe,
inevitable changes that will lead to a better, gentler, and truly
peaceful future.

Discovering Contemplative Spirituality

"America is discovering the contemplative life." These words
were written by Thomas Merton in his best-selling autobiography *The Seven Storey Mountain* (p. 414), published nearly fifty
years ago. They were true then; they are even truer today.
There is a hunger in people for a deeper dimension in their
lives and more and more women and men are finding it in contemplation. Spiritual direction has become a thriving ministry,
as more and more people look for help in discovering what is
going on inside of them and interpreting what God is doing in
their lives. Contemplative spirituality is alive in a way perhaps
that it has never been before.

Discovery of Nonviolence

Christians are discovering in the scriptures Jesus' call to nonviolence. The leaven of nonviolence continues steadily and
tirelessly to spread its transforming power wherever it can
reach. The Fellowship of Reconciliation is much better known
and respected than it was, say, in the 1960s. It was in 1962 that
Thomas Merton became the first or one of the first Catholics
to join the FOR.

Based at Nyack, New York, and affiliated with the International Fellowship (whose offices are in Holland), the Fellowship of Reconciliation is open to people of various religious
traditions. With a history that covers most of this century, it
has branches all over the country dedicated to dealing with all
sorts of conflict situations in a nonviolent way.

Among Catholics, who have clung so tenaciously to the just

war theory, the growth of nonviolence has been slow. With Daniel and Philip Berrigan, James Forest, Thomas Cornell, and others, Merton would have liked to set up an American chapter of Pax Christi International (whose headquarters are in Brussels). But in the 1960s it was impossible to organize a Pax Christi, USA. The reason was simple. One of the rules of Pax Christi is that its president must be a bishop. In the 1960s there were no American bishops who would have dared to assume such a position, even if they might be inclined to do so. It was the age of Cardinal Francis Spellman and Catholic bellicosity. Roman Catholics, including the Roman Catholic hierarchy, were strongly patriotic. I recall sometime in the 1960s hearing a bishop quote approvingly, in a public talk, the words of Stephen Decatur, a naval officer in the war of 1812, who said: "Our country . . . may she always be in the right. But our country right or wrong." No Catholic bishop would dare voice such sentiments today, even if he might think them. Indeed, the pastoral letter of the American bishops "The Challenge of Peace," issued in 1983, offered nonviolence as an alternative to the just war theory. This was a huge breakthrough in American Catholic thought.

Fifteen years before the publication of that pastoral Thomas Gumbleton was ordained auxiliary bishop of Detroit. And it was no accident that four years after his episcopal ordination, in the year 1972, Pax Christi, USA, came into existence, with Gumbleton as its first president. Pax Christi has chapters throughout the United States and continues to grow and to spread the message of nonviolence through publications, actions, conventions, and whatever other means it has at its disposal. It is a force to be reckoned with in the Catholic Church in the United States.

Somalia

In 1992, the year that Pax Christi was celebrating its twentieth anniversary, the United States government offered its ser-

vices to safeguard the delivery of food to people starving in
Somalia. One of the tasks the American "peacemaking force"
had to deal with in Somalia was the sponsoring of negotiations
among rival warlords seeking to seize power in their country.

Whom did we have available for carrying out this most sensitive mission? Unfortunately the only group available in large
numbers to carry out this task was United States military
personnel. To help make peace we had only people whose
training had been to make war. The result of this well-meaning
effort on the part of our government was mediocre success in
distributing food and dismal failure in our efforts to promote
negotiations among various factions that divided a hapless
country vainly yearning for peace.

Let's Have a Dream

Let us try to imagine a different scenario. Suppose that,
instead of sending to Somalia ten thousand soldiers, whose
business is to make war, we had been able to send ten thousand
people trained in the principles and techniques of nonviolence. Would the results have been different? We have no way
of knowing for sure. But we can say that the very different way
in which nonviolence operates would give us good reasons to
expect that the results might have been very different.

But you will say: "We don't have ten thousand people trained
in nonviolence." The obvious response is: "We ought to have
them." Let us dream a moment. Suppose half the money bud-
geted for military expenditures were put to use to train people
for making peace through nonviolent means. Suppose half of
the money spent on armaments went to the Fellowship of Reconciliation, Pax Christi, USA, and similar peace-making
groups. Would it then be possible for us, as we bring our century to a close, to do away with war, as the last century did away
with slavery? Could the year 2001 usher in a century that would
be free from war, a century in which the peace that *shalom*
embodies would cast its bright light all over the world?

This is a dream: a dream of a world of transformed hearts, a dream of a new world order in which justice, equality, and peace would prevail and in which people would truly care for one another. Such a dream could be like a castle in the sand that would crumble easily in the face of reality; or it could be a vision of a better future calling us and moving us to live in communion and to reach out to one another in caring concern. A vision of this sort is rooted in a contemplative intuition, for it sees that we are all one with one another. It tells us that we have to be what we are.

But the dream cannot be just your dream or mine. We must all dream together, as we must all work together to make the dream a reality. As Dom Helder Camara, a convert to nonviolence, put it: "When we dream alone, it is only a dream. When we dream together it is the beginning of reality."

New Testament Readings on Peace

¶

Blessed are the peacemakers, for they will be called the children of God. (Matthew 5:5)

Be at peace with one another. (Mark 9:50)

By the tender mercy of our God, the dawn from on high will break upon us . . . to guide our feet into the way of peace. (Luke 1:79)

Glory to God in the highest heaven and on earth peace among those whom he favors. (Luke 2:14)

Your faith has saved you; go in peace. (Luke 7:50)

If you, even you, had only recognized on this day the things that make for peace! But now they are hidden from your eyes. (Luke 19:42)

Peace I leave with you; my peace I give you. (John 14:27)

I have said this to you, so that in me you may have peace. (John 16:33)

Jesus came and stood among them and said, "Peace be with you." (John 20:19)

You know the message [God] sent to the people of Israel, preaching peace by Jesus Christ—he is Lord of all. (Acts 10:36)

Grace to you and peace from God our Father and the Lord Jesus Christ. (Romans 1:7)

Therefore, since we are justified by faith, we have peace with God through our Lord Jesus Christ, through whom we have obtained access to this grace in which we stand. (Romans 5:1, 2)

For the kingdom of God is not food and drink but righteousness and peace and joy in the Holy Spirit. (Romans 14:17)

Let us then pursue what makes for peace and for mutual upbuilding. (Romans 14:19)

May the God of hope fill you with all joy and peace in believing, so that you may abound in hope by the power of the Holy Spirit. (Romans 15:13)

The God of peace be with all of you. Amen. (Romans 15:33)

It is to peace that God has called you. (1 Corinthians 7:15)

For God is a God not of disorder but of peace. (1 Corinthians 14:33)

Brothers and sisters . . . agree with one another, live in peace; and the God of love and peace will be with you. (2 Corinthians 13:11)

The fruit of the Spirit is love, joy, peace, patience, kindness, generosity, faithfulness, gentleness and self-control. (Galatians 5:22)

But now in Christ Jesus you who once were far off have been brought near by the blood of Christ. For he is our peace; in his flesh he has made both groups into one and has broken down the dividing wall, that is the hostility between us. He has abolished the law with its commands and ordinances, that he might create in himself one new humanity in place of the two, thus making peace, and might reconcile both groups to God in one body through the cross, thus putting to death that hostility through it. So he came and proclaimed peace to you who were far off and peace to those who were near; for through him both of us have access in one Spirit to the Father. (Ephesians 2:13–18)

I beg you to lead a life worthy of the calling to which you have been called, with humility and gentleness, with patience, bearing with one another in love, making every effort to maintain the unity of the Spirit in the bond of peace. (Ephesians 4:1–3)

. . . Put on whatever will make you ready to proclaim the gospel of peace. (Ephesians 6:15)

Peace to the whole community, and love with faith from God the Father and the Lord Jesus Christ. (Ephesians 6:23)

The peace of God, which surpasses all understanding, will guard your hearts and your minds in Christ Jesus. . . . Keep on doing the things that you have learned and received and heard and seen in me, and the God of peace will be with you. (Philippians. 4:7, 9)

For in him all the fullness of God was pleased to dwell, and through him God was pleased to reconcile to himself all things, whether on earth or in heaven, by making peace through the blood of his cross. (Colossians 1:19–20)

Let the peace of Christ rule in your heart. (Colossians 3:15)

Be at peace among yourselves. (1 Thessalonians 5:13)

May the God of peace himself sanctify you entirely. (1 Thessalonians 5:23)

Now may the Lord of peace himself give you peace at all times in all ways. (2 Thessalonians 3:16)

Pursue peace with everyone, and the holiness without which no one will see God. (Hebrews 12:14)

A harvest of righteousness is sown in peace for those who make peace. (James 3:18)

Peace to all of you who are in Christ. (1 Peter 5:14)

—NRSV

Works Cited

§

Houver, Gerard. *A Non-Violent Lifestyle: Converersations with Jean and Hildegard Goss-Mayr.* Trans. Richard Bateman. London: Lamp Press, 1989.

James, William. *The Varieties of Religious Experience: A Study in Human Nature.* New York: Collier-Macmillan, 1961.

Jesudasan, Ignatius. *A Gandhian Theology of Liberation.* Maryknoll: NY: Orbis, 1984.

King, Martin Luther, Jr. *Stride toward Freedom.* New York: Harper & Row (Perennial Library edition), 1964 (original edition, 1958).

——. *A Testament of Hope: The Essential Writings and Speeches of Martin Luther King, Jr.* Ed. James M. Washington. San Francisco: HarperCollins, 1991.

Merton, Thomas. *The Asian Journal of Thomas Merton.* Ed. Naomi Stone, Patrick Hart, and James Laughlin. New York: New Directions, 1973. Cited as *AJ.*

——. *Conjectures of a Guilty Bystander.* New York: Doubleday, 1966. Cited as *CGB.*

——. *Collected Poems.* New York: New Directions, 1977. Cited as *CP.*

——. *Contemplative Prayer.* New York: Herder & Herder, 1969. Cited as *CPR.*

——. *Contemplation in a World of Action.* New York: Doubleday Image, 1973. Cited as *CWA.*

——. *Disputed Questions.* New York: Farrar Straus and Cuhady, 1960. Cited as *DQ.*

——. *Gandhi on Non-Violence.* New York: New Directions, 1965. Cited as *GNV.*

——. *The Hidden Ground of Love: Letters on Religious Experience and Social Concerns.* Ed. William H. Shannon. New York: Farrar, Straus and Giroux, 1985. Cited as *HGL.*

——. *Love and Living.* Ed. Naomi Burton Stone and Patrick Hart. New York: Farrar Straus and Giroux, 1979. Cited as *LL.*

——. *The New Man.* New York: Farrar Straus and Cudahy, 1961. Cited as *NM.*

——. *New Seeds of Contemplation.* New York: New Directions, 1962. Cited as *NSC.*

——. *No Man Is an Island.* New York: Harcourt Brace, 1955. Cited as *NMII.*

——. *Passion for Peace: The Social Essays of Thomas Merton.* Ed. and with an intro. by William H. Shannon. New York: Crossroad, 1995. Cited as *PFP.*

——. *The Road to Joy: Letters to New and Old Friends.* Ed. Robert E. Daggy. New York: Farrar Straus and Giroux, 1989. Cited as *RJ.*

——. *Raids on the Unspeakable.* New York: New Directions, 1966. Cited as *RU.*

——. *The School of Charity: Letters on Religious Renewal and Spiritual Direction.* Ed. Patrick Hart. New York: Farrar Straus and Giroux, 1990. Cited as *SC.*

——. *The Sign of Jonas.* New York: Harcourt Brace, 1953. Cited as *SJ.*

——. *The Seven Storey Mountain.* New York: Harcourt Brace, 1948. Cited as *SSM.*

——. *The Tears of the Blind Lions.* New York: New Directions, 1949. Cited as *TBL.*

——. *Thoughts in Solitude.* New York: Farrar Straus and Cudahy, 1958. Cited as *TIS.*

——. *Witness to Freedom: Letters in Times of Crisis.* Ed. William H. Shannon. New York: Farrar Straus and Giroux, 1994. Cited as *WTF.*

———. *What Are These Wounds?* Milwaukee: Bruce, 1950. Cited as *WTW.*

Shannon, William H. *Seeking the Face of God.* New York: Crossroad, 1988.

———. *Silence on Fire.* New York: Crossroad, 1991.

Sharp, Gene. *The Politics of Nonviolent Action.* Boston: Porter Sargent, 1972–1973. Part One: *Power and Struggle;* Part Two: *The Dynamics of Nonviolent Action.* Part Three: *The Methods of Nonviolent Action.*

Vanderhaar, Gerard A. *Active Non-Violence: A Way of Personal Peace.* Mystic, CT: Twenty-Third Publications, 1990.